Creative Chess

(Expanded Edition)

CADOGAN CHESS SERIES

Chief Adviser: Garry Kasparov
Editor: Murray Chandler
Russian Series Editor: Ken Neat

Other titles available from Cadogan include:

THE SORCERER'S APPRENTICE
Bronstein & Furstenberg

FIRE ON BOARD:
SHIROV'S BEST GAMES
Alexei Shirov

IVAN SOKOLOV'S BEST GAMES
Ivan Sokolov

ENDGAME VIRTUOSO
Vassily Smyslov

TAIMANOV'S SELECTED GAMES
Mark Taimanov

THE LIFE AND GAMES
OF MIKHAIL TAL
Mikhail Tal

PLAY THE EVANS GAMBIT
Harding and Cafferty

DANGER IN CHESS
Amatzia Avni

THE FINAL COUNTDOWN
Hajenius and van Riemsdijk

KING'S INDIAN DEFENCE:
AVERBAKH VARIATION
Margeir Petursson

QUEEN'S INDIAN DEFENCE
Bogdan Lalic

QUEEN'S GAMBIT ACCEPTED
Iakov Neishtadt

PLAY THE NOTEBOOM
Van der Werf and Van der Vorm

PRACTICAL ENDGAME PLAY
Neil McDonald

For a complete catalogue of CADOGAN CHESS books
(which includes the former Pergamon Chess and
Maxwell Macmillan Chess list) please write to:
Cadogan Books, 3rd Floor, 27-29 Berwick St, London W1V 3RF

Creative Chess

(Expanded Edition)

by
Amatzia Avni

Translated by
Simon Kay

CADOGAN
chess
LONDON, NEW YORK

First published 1991 by Pergamon Press Books plc, as *Creative Chess*

This expanded edition published 1997 by Cadogan Books Plc,
27-29 Berwick St, London W1V 3RF

British Library Cataloguing in Publication Data
A CIP catalogue record for this book is available from the British Library

ISBN 1 85744 149 4

Distributed in North America by Simon & Schuster, Paramount Publishing,
200 Old Tappan Road, Old Tappan, New Jersey 07675, USA.

All other sales enquiries should be directed to Cadogan Books plc,
27-29 Berwick St, London W1V 3RF

Cover by Berfort Reproductions
Typesetting by A-Type, Ripponden
Printed and bound in Great Britain by BPC Wheatons Ltd, Exeter

Contents

Introduction to the Expanded Edition

In mid-1987 I gave lectures to several groups of chess players. The groups were heterogenous; they included youths and adults, students and trainers, from relatively weak club-players up to 2300 national masters. For my talks I chose some fascinating, out-of-the-ordinary positions, and assembled them under the headline "creative chess".

This was the modest beginning of this book.

One of the examples I cited was the following

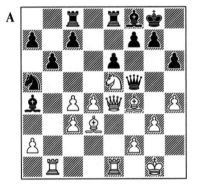

In this position (No. 12 in this book), White decides the outcome with **1 ♕h1!**

I've noticed that the strongest participants in the lectures solved this puzzle within seconds; while others stared at the demonstration board for some minutes without success.

I was intrigued; after all, everyone attending had been told that there existed a solution, a forced win. So, why did some players fail to reach it?

I could think of three plausible explanations (a fourth — overlooking the availability of a decisive continuation — does not apply here, since the participants had been told that such a continuation existed):

A) The position is rife with possibilities (i.e. with many logical "candidate moves").

B) The position requires lengthy calculations, perhaps six or eight moves deep.

C) The calculation required involves unforced play, and there are numerous side-variations.

Option A taxes one's perception; Options B and C burden one's memory, thus making it difficult for a player to accomplish the task.

Now, none of these explanations applies to diagram A.

The number of candidate-moves is limited; obviously, White has to start with his queen. The correct line is only three moves deep, it is of a forced nature, and there is only one side-variation (1 ... ♕h5) which is refuted by a one-mover.

So why the difficulty, I wondered.

In one of the groups, trying to assist my public, I gave them a hint: "Think of an unusual queen-move".

There was silence, and then a young participant said loudly, in jest: "Aha! 1 ♕a8 !"

There was some laughter. I queried: "Why not 1 ♕h1 ?"

"Well", said the trainee, "1 ♕a8, 1 ♕h1 — it's the same." (!)

This made me think. Apparently some moves, some pieces, some squares do not enter many players' thinking process: the move 1 ♕h1 *was not considered at all*. Relegating the strongest piece to such a humble square was a *non-existent* alternative for them, unthinkable as 1 ♕a8. Not that it was a remote possibility; it was not an option at all, as if the move was illegal.

Later I came to think that chess players develop in three stages. In the first, when the newcomer learns the rules, every move is perceived as possible. In the previous diagram, for example, moves like h5, ♔g2, ♗e2 or ♕h1 all make sense to the beginner's mind, and are examined with equal attention and seriousness.

In the second stage, the player acquires principles and stratagems; he learns that in position X the right plan is Y; that in positions of type Z it is wrong to trade one's bishop for a knight; that in all variations of opening T, one should castle on the queen-side, etc.

This is a vital step in a chessplayer's development. He learns to place things in categories, to ascertain priorities. It makes his thinking process more ordered, economical and efficient.

There is a danger, though. A chessplayer might miss the *exception* to the rules. He may be blind to ♕h1-moves, since they do not fall into the usual categories, do not fit in the frames that he created.

To become an all-round player, a third integrative stage of development is essential. That is, to understand general principles, but also to be able to detect exceptions; to see the frame, but to be sensitive to what lies outside it.

Stage one	Stage two	Stage three
Everything may be right; everything is possible. There are no principles, no guiding laws.	Everything that falls inside the frames is possible; the rest is wrong.	Everything that falls inside the frames is possible; the boundaries between the frames and their surroundings are not rigid. So what is outside the frames can *also* be possible.

I believe that many chess players get stuck after reaching stage two. Unable to perceive uncommon ideas, they fail to realise their full potential.

Hopefully, working through the examples in this book will facilitate the reader's journey to the third stage!

This expanded edition contains corrections of some errors in the original manuscript that were brought to my attention; minor textual changes, and also new chapters incorporating creative ideas.

Amatzia Avni
Ramat-Ilan, Israel
August 1997

Introduction to the First Edition

The origins of chess lie in deep antiquity. In its present form the game has been played for centuries by hundreds of millions and intensively investigated. It could be said that in our time the scope for innovative and sensational discovery has been reduced, even considering the enormous possibilities open to the player. Chess has become a technical game, entailing more knowledge and less creativity and imagination than in the past. In fact we seldom see a game, or even a part thereof (a scheme, or an endgame) displaying fresh originality. Most games give us an impression of *déja vu*, i.e. we've seen it all before and nothing new is apparent.

Several (outstanding) players have suggested a change in some of the principles of the game e.g. an extension of the board, introduction of some new pieces with new moves, modifying the starting positions of the new pieces etc. However, none of these ideas has found more than a few supporters, and the rules have remained unchanged.[1]

Many thinkers debate the old philosophical question about the nature of chess — is it a science, an art or a sport? Prevailing opinion nowadays regards chess as a sport.[2, 3] Most grandmasters in modern times consider it to be their profession, hence victory (and the consequent improvement in their score, acquiring rating points and pecuniary gain) overrules any desire to create and innovate. Well known and tested systems pay better than adventurous ideas, with all their uncertainty, and so innovation does not blossom any more as in the past. Moreover, chessplayers' motivation to invent, innovate and change has been diminishing. With this lack of ability and will to change, are the pessimists right, and do we approach the 'death' of the *Royal Game*?

This book presents a collection of exceptional chess ideas — odd, bizarre, non-routine, and seemingly illogical. Most chess books aim to enrich their readers with 'know-how'. They produce principles, rules, schemes, methods of play and theories. The present book differs by stressing a peculiar and original *way of thinking*: creative thinking in chess.

It is the author's belief that every chess player, be he an amateur or a master, is still capable of creating something new in chess, if only he so wishes. There is no reason to suppose that creative thinking should remain the faculty of the few. *Creativity can be developed.* The first step must be the widening of one's horizons in the method of problem-solving, and enlarging the range of available possibilities. We hope this work will assist the reader in this task.

1
Creativity in Chess

Guilford[4] developed the distinction between *convergent* and *divergent* thinking. The former takes place when we face a well defined problem having a standard method of solution (sometimes even known in advance) which leads to a single correct solution. The intellectual activity required from the thinker is memory and some understanding. Divergent thinking, on the other hand, is multi-dimensional. It is less restricted by the given facts and permits changes of direction in problem-solving which in turn, can lead to a diversity of solutions or products.

Examples of the first type of thinking include simple mathematical problems – "How long does it take to reach point B from point A at 40 m.p.h. by the shortest route?" The method of solution is clear, well defined and leads to a single correct answer.

Questions like, "What are the possible uses of empty tins?", "What will happen if it starts raining tomorrow and never stops?", or "Which objects can change their form to round without endangering their function?", demand divergent thinking. There are no "correct" answers as such and one can use various ways of reasoning to arrive at diverse answers.

Summarising the basic differences, Guilford concluded that convergent thinking is the type of reasoning examined in common Intelligence Tests, while branched, divergent thinking is characteristic of creativity.

Characteristics of the creative process

Psychologists are agreed that creativity is a process, whereby something new, an idea or a product – interesting and/or valuable – is produced. The act of creation is not taken for granted and it frequently evokes expressions of surprise and even veneration: "How did he think of that?" "How did she manage to do it?" However it is erroneous to assume that creative innovation is derived from divine

1

inspiration; rather, the creative process starts with the reorganisation of already existing elements. Simon[5] claims that creativity is based on a good problem-solving capability, and that effort, know-how and skill are *conditio-sine-qua-non* of the development of the creative process.

Psychological research shows that creative people are distinguished, *inter alia*, by the following characteristics: being sensitive to change and ready to respond to it even if it means discarding well prepared programmes; being highly tolerant of ambiguity; a willingness to take risks; and the ability to approach problems by non-conformist methods[6].

In the process of creation, four central stages can be identified and differentiated.[6,16].

In the **preparation** phase, raw material, bearing on the subject, is gathered. Immersed in information, no distinction is made between the 'relevant' and the 'irrelevant'.

In the **incubation** stage, the material is thoroughly examined and subconsciously processed. Ideas are formed.

In the third stage an **enlightenment** occurs. In the course of the search for a solution to a problem one penetrates to the very core of the matter in great depth, and then, somewhere along the line, an 'insight' or 'brainwave' occurs as a solution.

All that remains is the **verification** stage, to examine the idea's value and transpose it from theory to reality.

Fischer-Sherwin
USA (ch), 1957

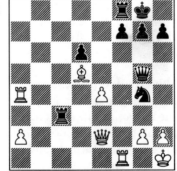

White to play

In order to demonstrate how creative thinking in chess works in practice, we will now try to describe the White player's train of thought in diagram 1.

In the preparation stage White gathers all the possible information. He examines the position of the pieces, makes a mental note of the weak and strong points of both sides, designs feasible short-term plans (for instance, pressure on the f7 pawn) and long-term plans (for example, advance of the a-pawn).

In the incubation stage, White examines several variants in a careful step by step manner. Let's assume that the moves 1 ♗xf7 + or 1 ♖xf7 catch his eye; he would go on analysing and soon see that after 1 ♗xf7+ ♔h8, the white bishop cannot move because of 2 ... ♖c1! and that he would also be in trouble after 1 ♖xf7 ♖c1+ 2 ♖f1+ ♔h8!.

Finally enlightenment occurs and he 'conceives' the idea 1 ♖xf7 ♖c1+ 2 ♕f1!!, going on to win!

All there is for White to do now is to verify the correctness of his idea, and after being convinced that his calculations are correct, he should implement it on the chessboard. The game continued: **1 ♖xf7!** **♖c1+** If 1 ... ♕xd5!? then 2 ♖xf8+ ♔xf8 3 ♕f1+! ♕f7 4 ♖a8+. **2 ♕f1!!** **h5** – or 2 ... ♖xf1+ 3 ♖xf1+ ♕xd5 4 ♖xf8+. **3 ♕xc1!** Stronger than 3 ♖xf8++ ♔h7. **3 ... ♕h4** Despair. 3 ... ♕xc1+ 4 ♖f1+ and 5 ♖xc1. **4 ♖xf8++ ♔h7 5 h3 ♕g3 6 hxg4 h4 7 ♗e6 Black resigns.**

A major obstacle to creativity is conformity: the inclination to be in the mainstream, to behave and act according to prevailing norms, and the fear of being regarded as a deviant. In diagram 1, Fischer had to liberate himself from the conception, "You do not place the queen where it can be captured", (especially when the loss of the queen is simultaneously bound up with check!) in order to arrive at the idea 2 ♕f1!!

The Elements of Chess Creativity

The notion of introducing system, organisation and order into a concept which, by definition, is opposed to system, organisation and order, seems paradoxical. Nevertheless, this book is divided into *categories* according to subjects. This is for two reasons. Firstly, *all* chess books are similarly constructed and the reader might face some difficulty in adapting himself to a different organisation of text. And secondly, as hinted before, there is a logic in this madness. Creativity is not such a mysterious, non-consequent and unfathomable process as it appears to many people (we shall return to this matter later).

Ten central concepts, characteristic of creative thinking in chess, will be discussed in the following chapters, namely:

A. **Unusual positioning of pieces;** sophisticated utilisation of the corner squares; placing pieces in passive positions based on long-term considerations; an original examination of the notion of retreat in chess.

B. **Unusual functioning of pieces;** employment of 'heavy' pieces for 'light' tasks; unconventional development of pieces; use of the king's potential as an attacking piece.

C. **Flexibility;** openness to change; readiness to deviate from the original plan; taking advantage of opportunities coming your way.

D. **Goal-orientated thinking;** long-term planning; focussing on the question, "where should the pieces ultimately be located?", with no reference to where they are at a certain time.

E. **Removal of your own piece;** recognising the situations where you have to get rid of your own pieces and not those of the opponent; reviewing the ways of removing them; turning hindering pieces into helping ones.

F. **Reducing the importance of the time element;** designing and carrying out long-term plans of unavoidable, albeit slow, maturing power.

G. **Alertness to subtle differences;** diagnosis of minor and subtle changes in the positioning of pieces; recognition of the importance of move order and of the different possibilities inherent sometimes in seemingly identical positions.

H. **Continuing calculation in a state of certainty;** scepticism and doubt even in 'certain' situations; tendency not to accept things as self-evident; probing and double checking.

I. **Violation of theoretical principles;** voluntarily entering a pin; intentional weakening of pawn formations; giving up castling rights; initiating an exchange of pieces while being materially inferior.

J. **Absurd moves;** exploring moves which seem to contradict chess logic; placing pieces in undefended positions; material sacrifices followed by quiet moves; sacrificing a piece lost with (simultaneous) check.

The book's concluding chapters contain a discussion of the essence of creativity in chess and its sources, a list of techniques for developing chess creativity, demonstrations of particularly creative games and a set of exercise positions for the benefit of the student chess player.

2
Unusual Positioning of Pieces

In principle the placing of pieces on the edges of the board is not recommended, since such positioning reduces their effectiveness and overall influence. The knight placed at a1 can only move to two squares whilst its counterpart placed in the middle of the board has eight possible moves. In a similar fashion, the bishop at a2 can move to seven squares whilst the same bishop, if positioned on a central square such as d5, can control 13 squares.

What then, if anything, can persuade a competent player to position his pieces on so called remote and unattractive squares?

I. Penetrating into the enemy's camp.

In chess, as in a battle, it is not customary to send forward an attacking force without any support from the rear. The penetration of a single piece into enemy territory without any back up support or routes of retreat often entails the loss of the attacking piece.

Pulykis-Zhuravlev
USSR, 1970

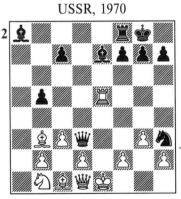

Black to play

6

However, as always, there are exceptions to the rule ... the invasion of a small force can sometimes decide the fate of the game.

From diagram 2, Black wins quickly after **1 ... ♗g2! 2 ♖e2 2 ♕e2? ♕xb1 2 ... ♘g1!** Simple, but aesthetically very pleasing. **3 f4 ♗c5 White resigns.**

Augustin-Lanč
Czechoslovakia, 1975.

White to play

White would certainly be happy to exchange the positions of his queen and his bishop, thereby threatening mate on d7. From here he develops the idea of using the battery in an unusual fashion **1 ♗e8!!** The two exclamation marks may look like exaggerated enthusiasm, but it is in fact surprising quite how strong this move really is. **1 ... ♕f5 2 ♖e6! Black resigns.** 2 ...♔c7 3 ♕d7+ leads to a quick mate.

From diagram 4 Black's last move was ... b5-b4, attacking the white knight which is apparently forced to retreat to its home square, b1. However, White thinks differently. **1 ♘a4!! ♕c6 2 ♘a5 ♕xa4 3 ♘xb7 ♕c6** It looks as though White has fallen straight into a trap: after 4 ♘a5 ♕c5! he must play the awkward 5 ♗d8?! to save a piece.

4 ♘d8! A remarkable position for a white knight at such an early stage of the game. From d8 the knight helps to put pressure on Black's Achilles heel — the f7 pawn. **4 ... ♕c7 5 ♗h5! g6 6 ♕f3 d6.** The White attack develops with gathering momentum. On 6 ...f6, 7 e5! is strong. **7 ♗g4 h6 8 ♗h4 ♗g7 8 ... g5? 9 ♘xf7! ♕xf7 10 ♗h5. 9 e5 d5 10 ♗xe6 fxe6 11 ♘xe6 ♕b7 12 ♘xg7+ ♕xg7 13 ♕xd5** and **White won** quickly.

Shamkovich-Marchand
New York, 1977

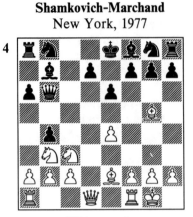

White to play

Domnitz-Rupin
Israel (ch), 1961-2

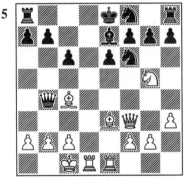

White to play

1 ♗a6!? Although strange from a positional point of view, this move has a sound tactical basis. White threatens 2 a3 and on the retreat of the queen the b-pawn will fall. 1 ... bxa6? loses to 2 ♕xc6+, of course, while 1 ... ♖b8 is also seen to be inadequate because of 2 a3 ♕a4 3 ♗f4!

1 ... ♖c8! 2 a3 ♕a4 3 ♗xb7 ♖c7 4 ♗a8.

White has achieved his aim but at a high price – the white bishop is stranded at the edge of the board with no retreat. However, as will become apparent, attempts to capture the bishop allow White to launch a strong attack on the king's wing.

4 ... ♘g6 4 ... ♕a6!? is probably better with the threat of 5 ... ♖c8. **5 ♖d4 ♕b5 6 h4! 0-0** On 6 ... ♖c8 White continues in similar fashion. **7 a4 ♕a6 8 h5 ♘h8** On 8 ... ♘e5 9 ♕g3 ♘fd7 10 h6 g6 11 ♖xd7 wins. **9 h6 g6** After 9 ... ♖xa8 10 hxg7 ♘g6 11 ♖h1, White develops a decisive attack, e.g., 11 ... ♖d8 12 ♘xh7 ♘xh7 13 ♕h5.

10 ♗f4 ♖7c8 11 ♗e5? Here White misses an opportunity to decide the battle by 11 ♗d6! and now 11 ... ♗xd6 12 ♕xf6, or 11 ... ♗d8 12 ♗xf8 intending 13 ♖xd8! winning immediately.

11 ... ♘d5 12 ♖xd5 ♗xg5+ 13 ♗f4 cxd5 14 ♗xg5 f5?! 15 ♖xe6 ♕f1+ 16 ♔d2 ♖xa8 17 ♕xd5 and, after further adventures, **White won.**

II. Intentionally placing a piece in an inferior position

Porreca-D. Bronstein
Belgrade, 1954

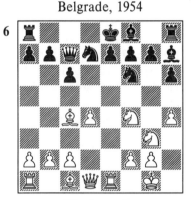

Black to play

Black is faced with serious difficulties in this position. Queenside castling is impossible because of 2 ♗xf7, and the preliminary 1 ... e6 will be answered by 2 ♗xe6 with a decisive attack. Even the continuation 1 ... ♘b6 2 ♗b3 ♘bd5 3 ♕f3 does not guarantee Black an easy time. On that note it's possible to anticipate the continuation **1 ... ♗g8!**

An awkward move? Yes, but it does allow Black to finish developing (2 ... 0-0-0, 3 ... e6, etc). Bronstein was successful in gradually unravelling his position.

Miles-Makarichev
Oslo, 1984

White to play

In diagram 7, White surprised his opponent with **1 ♘h1!**

The reason for this strange move, placing the knight on a square from which it can only return to the square it moved from, is based on the fact that the alternatives, 1 ♕c6 ♗xg3 and 1 ♘f1 ♕b2, give Black counterplay. Even though the last move neutralises the knight, the extra protection afforded to f2 gives the white queen a free hand to operate against the black pawns. **1 ... ♕b2** If 1 ... ♗e7 2 ♕c6 ♗d6 3 ♘g3! intending 4 ♘e4. **2 ♕c6 ♕b1 3 ♕xc7 ♕e4+ 4 ♔h2 h5 5 ♕c6! ♕c2 6 gxh5 ♕f5 7 ♕g2 ♕xh5 8 c5! and White wins.** Although White's pieces are in "poor" positions, his advantage on the queen's flank determines the result of the battle.

In diagram 8, **1 ♖a2!** Could this be a good move? Or is a weak player playing White ... and how could he place a proud rook on a square so lacking in influence, just for the passive protection of a mere pawn? Isn't that how things appear?

An accurate analysis reveals that White has a formidable attack on the king's flank where he threatens the pawn thrust g2-g4-g5. For that purpose the rook is required to remain on h1 and thus the king remains in the centre. A certain level of caution is still required to avoid any unpleasantries, and the white rook at a2 proves to be an effective defender. The obvious move, 1 b4 would have given Black some counter-chances after 1 ... ♖ac8 with the threat 2 ... ♘xb4 3 axb4 ♖xc3!; for example 1 b4 ♖ac8 2 ♘a4? ♘xb4! etc.

Lipnitsky-Smyslov
USSR (ch), 1950

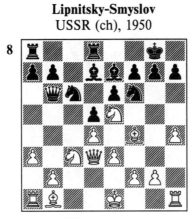

White to play

After the move played, Black is denied any counter chances. **1 ... ♔f8
2 g4 ♘xe5 3 dxe5 ♘e4 4 f3! ♘xc3 5 ♕xh7 ♔e8 6 bxc3 ♖dc8 7 ♔f2**
White's material and positional advantages were decisive.

The three examples given above all had a common denominator: one piece was positioned badly to enable the other pieces to perform to the best of their abilities, and at the same time prevent the opponent from developing counterplay. In the following positions we will discover other ideas involving the placing of a piece on an inferior square, namely the prevention of an exchange of pieces (Diagram 9), gaining a material advantage (Diagram 10) and a quick changeover from defence to attack (Diagram 11).

1 ♗a7! This block on the a-file prevents an exchange of rooks. White is planning to double his rooks on the a-file and then, after pulling back the bishop, gain control of the file.

**1 ... ♘e8 2 ♗c2 ♘c7 3 ♖ea1 ♕e7 4 ♗b1 ♗e8 5 ♘e2 ♘d8 6 ♘h2 ♗g7
7 f4 f6 8 f5 g5 9 ♗c2 ♗f7 10 ♘g3.**

White has gained a decisive advantage and over the following moves he will concentrate his force on the king's flank, knowing full well that if the need arises he can always come back and apply pressure on the second front.

**10 ... ♘b7 11 ♗d1 h6 12 ♗h5 ♕e8 13 ♕d1 ♘d8 14 ♖a3 ♔f8 15 ♖1a2
♔g8 16 ♘g4 ♔f8 17 ♘e3 ♔g8 18 ♗xf7+ ♘xf7 19 ♕h5 ♘d8 20 ♕g6 ♔f8**

Karpov-Unzicker
Nice (ol), 1974

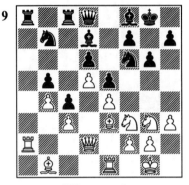

White to play

21 ♘h5 Black resigns.

After 21 ... ♕f7 22 ♘g4 ♘e8 23 ♗b6 the rooks penetrate via the a-file which White promised himself some 20 moves ago!

Villegas-Capablanca
Exhibition game, Buenos Aires, 1911

Black to play

1 ... ♖hg8! A mysterious move. What is the rook doing here? 2 c4 ♘f5 3 ♗xf5 gxf5 4 ♖dg1 ♗f6 5 ♔d2 ♖xg1 6 ♖xg1 ♖h8!

Again Black places his rook on a *closed* file. However, by doing this he wins the important h4-pawn, 7 ♖h1 being met very strongly by 7 ... ♖g8!

7 b4 ♗xh4 8 ♗d4 ♖h6 9 ♔e2 ♗e7 10 ♖g8+ ♔d7 11 ♔f3 h4 12 ♖g7 c5! 13 bxc5 dxc5 14 ♗e3 h3 15 ♖g1 b5 16 ♔e2 bxc4 17 ♔d2 ♔d6 18 ♔c3 ♔xd5 19 f3 ♗f6+ **White resigns.**

Grünfeld-Greenfeld
Israel (ch), 1984

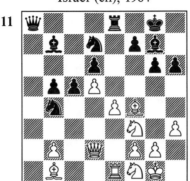

Black to play

Black has weak pawns on d6 and h6 and has to play aggressively to stand a fighting chance. **1 ... ♕a1!** Considering White's reply, this is a daring move, placing the black queen under an indirect threat from White's rook.

2 e5! ♘xe5 2 ... dxe5? 3 ♗f5 3 ♘xe5 dxe5 4 d6! Not 4 ♗xg6? ♕a8! and two white pieces are 'hanging'. **4 ... ♕a8! 5 d7 ♖d8 6 ♗xe5 ♘d5!** Not 6 ... ♗xg2? 7 ♗c7. **7 ♗xg7 ♔xg7 8 ♘e3 ♖xd7 9 ♘g4 ♕h8!**

The willingness of Black to station his strongest piece on distant squares, from where it has relatively little scope, is particularly striking. White could not gain any advantage against such superb defence.

10 ♗e4 h5 11 ♘e5 ♖d6 12 b4! cxb4 13 ♘xg6! fxg6 14 ♗xd5 ♗xd5 15 ♕d4+ ♖f6 16 ♕xd5 ♕f8 17 ♖c1!? ♕d6!? A double inaccuracy. After 17 ... ♖xf2 Black would be better. **Draw agreed.**

Apart from the last move, this game is a classic example of a strong attack meeting a calculated and cool headed defence which ended, quite rightly, with honours shared.

III. An attacking withdrawal

Don't the terms 'retreat' and 'attack' side by side seem like a logical contradiction? Can a chess player *retreat*, that is, withdraw, and at the same time *attack*, that is, be on the offensive? The answer is in the affirmative!

In diagram 12, White has an immediate and reasonably straight-forward win. Many chess players have difficulty in finding the winning move simply because they are unwilling to consider placing their queen in a compromised position such as ...

Filguth-De La Garza
Mexico, 1980

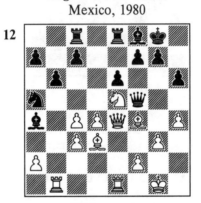

White to play

1 ♕h1!! Black resigns!

After 1 ... ♕f6 (1 ... ♕h5? 2 g4!) 2 ♗g5! hxg5 3 hxg5 Black is either mated or loses his queen.

In an apparently equal position (diagram 13), White forces an immediate win, based on a brilliant attacking withdrawal.

1 ♗d4+ ♗f6 2 ♗b2!!

Less good was 2 ♕c4 ♘d5! (3 ♕xc6 bxc6 4 ♗xd5 ♗xd4). The text move protects the first rank and creates two decisive threats: 3 ♕c4! and 3 ♕e7!

Black resigns. 2 ... ♗xb2 3 ♕xb2+, and 2 ... ♘e8 3 ♕xe8+! both lead to mate.

Riga-Oriol
City contest, USSR, 1896

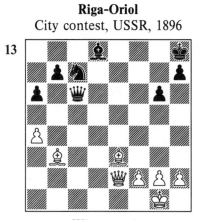

13

White to play

Nimzovitch-Rubinstein
Dresden, 1926

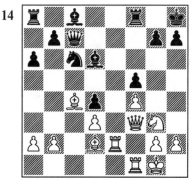

14

White to play

1 ♘h1! An extravagant but very effective move. White is planning a brilliant future for his knight on g5, and the beginning of the road is the square h1.

1 ... ♗d7 2 ♘f2 ♖ae8 3 ♖fe1 ♖xe2 4 ♖xe2 ♘d8 5 ♘h3 ♗c6 6 ♕h5 g6 7 ♕h4 ♔g7 8 ♕f2 ♗c5 9 b4 ♗b6 10 ♕h4 ♖e8 11 ♖e5! ♘f7 12 ♗xf7 ♕xf7 13 ♘g5

White accomplishes his mission and his advantage is beyond doubt.

13 ... ♕g8 14 ♖xe8 ♗xe8 15 ♕e1! ♗c6 16 ♕e7+ ♔h8 17 b5!

The winning move. 17 ... axb5 18 ♘e6 h5 19 ♕f6+ ♚h7 20 ♘g5+ ♚h6 21 ♗b4 and wins.

17 ... ♕g7 18 ♕xg7+ ♚xg7 19 bxc6 Black resigns.

IV. Voluntarily giving up castling

Castling is one of the most common moves in chess. The advantages yielded by castling — placing the king on a well protected square while simultaneously bringing a rook into play — are the reasons for its widespread application. Hence castling by both players occurs in the great majority of games.

The three following positions show one player deliberately giving up the right to castle, each instance displaying a certain logic under the specific circumstances. After all, castling is only a means to an end, not an end in itself.

Kovacevic-Seirawan
Wijk aan Zee, 1980

Black to play

1 ... ♚d7! The king will find himself a safe place on the queen's flank. His removal from the centre creates a link between the queen and the rook on g8, thereby allowing Black to make a bid for control of the h-file.

The game continued **2 ♘bd2 ♖h8 3 ♖g1 ♚c7 4 ♖b1 ♖h3 5 b3 ♕h8** Black took the initiative and won the game.

In diagram 16, a certain amount of caution is required by Black: **1 ...**

Klavin-Sokolsky
Minsk, 1957

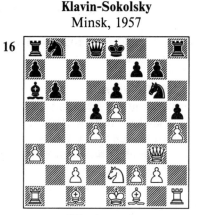

Black to play

♘c6? 2 ♘f4! is good for White, while 1 ... 0-0 2 ♕f3 is also unsatisfactory. Black finds an interesting way to reorganise his pieces.

1 ... ♔f8! 2 a4 ♕e8! The g6 square is now covered quite well and Black is able to finish off developing his queen's wing.

3 ♕g5 ♘d7 4 ♘f4 ♗xf1 5 ♘xg6+ fxg6 6 ♔xf1 a5 7 ♖h3 ♔g8 8 ♗a3 c5 9 ♖b1 ♔h7 10 ♖g3 ♖f8 11 ♕e3 ♖f5, with an advantage to Black, who eventually won.

Ivanovic-Sveshnikov
USSR, 1976

Black to play

In diagram 17 Black is faced with some serious problems in view of the threats 2 ♕c6+, and 2 ♗xf5. The Soviet Grandmaster finds an unusual solution.

1 ... e4! 2 ♕c6+ ♔e7 3 ♗xb5 ♖a7! 4 ♕e8+ ♔f6. As it turns out, the black king is quite well protected and it is in fact the *white* king which finds himself in trouble.

5 g4? ♖e7 6 ♕b8 ♔e5! 7 f4+ ♔xf4 Black's impunity drove White crazy, but in his attempts to attack he succeeds only in exposing his own king. **8 ♔e2 ♔e5 9 ♖hf1 fxg4 10 b4 ♗g7!** Not 10 ... ♕xb4? 11 ♖f5+! ♔xf5 12 ♗d7+, winning the queen. **11 bxa5** Entering a lost ending through lack of choice. 11 ♕xh8? ♕xb5+ loses immediately.

11 ... ♖xb8 12 ♖ab1 f5 13 a6 f4 14 ♗c6 f3+ 15 ♔f2 ♖xb1 16 ♖xb1 ♔f4 17 ♖b4 ♗c3 18 ♖c4 ♗a5 19 ♔f1 ♗b6 20 ♗b7 h5 21 ♖c6 otherwise the advance of the black g- and h-pawns will decide the issue.

21 ... e3! 22 ♖c4+ Or 22 ♖xb6 e2+ 23 ♔e1 f2+ etc. **22 ... ♔g5 White resigns.**

3
Unusual Functioning of Pieces

The experienced chess player knows the advantages and the limitations of the different pieces. The rook, for example, as he was taught, should be moved comparatively late in the game, after the other pieces have been developed. The king should be kept on a protected square; the queen should only be deployed for heavy duty tasks and should not be bothered with trifling matters such as the safeguarding of pawns; the knight is efficient in the role of blockading piece; and so on.

However, such rules of thumb are not absolute truths. In certain circumstances success is guaranteed to the player who develops independent and original criteria.

I. The King as an attacking piece

Hass-Diskin
Israel(ch; ½ Final), 1971

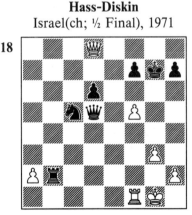

18

White to play

White has exposed Black's king at the cost of a piece and now he can gain a draw by perpetual check — 1 ♕g5+, 2 ♕d8+, and so on. In place

19

of this, he is tempted to carry on with his attack. **1 f6+? ♔h6 2 ♕f8+ ♔h5 3 g4+ ♔xg4 4 ♕g7+ ♕g5 5 ♔h1!**

White pins his hopes on this nice move. The following sequence shows that the black king is not ready merely to look after himself — he is also keen to demonstrate an aggressive streak.

5 ... ♘e4!! 6 h3+ or 6 ♖g1+ ♔f3 with the threat 7 ... ♘f2 mate, or 6 ♕xh7 ♘g3+ 7 hxg3 ♕d5+, and mates.

6 ... ♔g3 7 ♖g1+ ♔f3 8 ♕xg5 8 ♖xg5 is answered similarly.

8 ... ♘f2+ 9 ♔h2 ♘g4++ 10 ♔h1 ♖h2 mate!

Portisch-Pinter
Hungary (ch), 1984

19
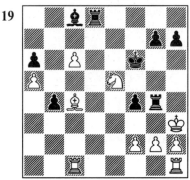

Black to play

1 ... ♔g5!! Threatening 2 ... ♖h4 mate, or 2 ... ♖g3 mate and naturally, 2 ♘xg4 induces mate by 2 ... ♗xg4. Instead of the last move, it would have been a mistake to play 1 ... ♔xe5? 2 ♖he1+ ♔f6 3 ♗e6! or 1 ... ♖g3++ 2 ♔h4 g5+ 3 ♔h5 with advantage to White.

2 ♘f7+ or 2 ♘f3+ ♔h6 3 ♖hd1 ♖g3+ 4 ♔h4 ♖xf3! and 5 ... g5 mate.

2 ... ♔h5 3 ♗e2 ♖d3+! 4 g3 or 4 ♗f3 ♖xf3+ 5 gxf3 ♖g3 mate. **4 ... f3!** Closing the net around the white king. 5 ♗xf3 ♖xf3 and 6 ... ♖xf7 is completely lost for White. Now follows an amusing series of checks.

5 ♖c5+ ♖g5+ 6 g4+ ♗xg4+ 7 ♔g3 fxe2+ White resigns.

In diagram 18, the black king was forced to set out on an adventurous journey. In the position shown in diagram 19, the black monarch was not safely placed, and its joining in the attack was dictated by the circumstances.

However this is not the case in the next position. The white king leaves its safe refuge, where it is unlikely to be in any danger, to embark onto a stormy sea ...

Teichmann-Consultants
Glasgow, 1902

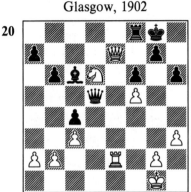

White to play

1 ♔h2!! Why should such a modest move be the subject of so much praise and respect? The answer lies in the idea behind the move — White intends to bring his king to g6(!) and then to finish off with ♕g7 mate. The idea appears not only crazy but also without a hope of success. Black, however, experiences surprising difficulty in preventing it.

1 ... b5 2 ♔g3 a5 3 ♔h4 g6 4 ♖e3! Obviously not 4 fxg6?? ♕g5 mate. But now, as a result of the king's march, there is no longer the threat of mate at g2; the white rook, freed from its defensive duties, rushes forward to bolster the attack.

4 ... ♕xg2 5 ♖g3 ♕f2 Or 5 ... g5+ 6 ♔h5 ♕xg3 7 ♔g6, and Black is mated. 6 fxg6 ♕f4+ 7 ♖g4 ♕f2+ 8 ♔h5 Black resigns.

II. Activating the rooks at an early stage

The position in diagram 21 developed from a quiet English Opening. We would have expected 1 0-0 followed by 2 a4 and 3 ♗a3, planning to strike in the centre with c4-c5 or d3-d4.

Instead of that, White chooses an original plan — he leaves his king in the centre and targets the a7 pawn.

Friedman-Mart
Israel (ch), 1972

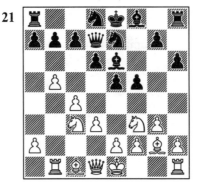

White to play

1 ♖b4! g5 2 ♖a4

It isn't an everyday occurrence to see a rook walking to and fro before the other pieces have developed. In the present position the manoeuvre is very effective. **2 ... ♗g7 3 ♕c2** Black intended 3 ... e4!

3 ... f4 4 ♗a3 ♘f5 5 g4! ♘d4 6 ♘xd4 exd4 7 ♘d5 0-0 7 ... c6? 8 ♘b6!

8 b6 reaping the fruits of his previous play. On 8 ... c6 comes 9 ♘c7 gaining material. **8 ... f3 9 ♗xf3 ♖xf3 10 exf3 ♗xd5 11 cxd5 cxb6 12 ♖c4**

White, without getting excited about his opponent's potential counterplay, continues to manoeuvre his rook skilfully.

12 ... ♘f7 13 ♖c7 ♖e8+ 14 ♔f1 ♕d8 15 ♗b2 ♕f6 16 ♖c8 ♖xc8 17 ♕xc8+ ♔h7 18 ♕f5+ ♕xf5 19 gxf5

White's material advantage was enough to win and after several moves **Black resigned.**

The strategy that is revealed in diagram 22 can be nicknamed 'the crazy rook'.

1 ... ♖b8 2 ♘c3!? 2 ♘d3 is preferable, preventing Black's next move. **2 ... ♖b4! 3 ♕a5 ♗b7 4 f3!? ♖h4!**

Whilst gaining a tempo with the threat 5 ... ♗b4, he brings his rook into an attacking position.

5 a3 ♖h5! 6 g4 ♘xg4!! 7 fxg4 ♖xh2!!

This rook, which only seven moves ago was on its original square, a8, is now creating havoc in White's camp. White does not have an adequate defence as is demonstrated by the following variations:

I. Shrentzel-Shvidler
Israel, 1985

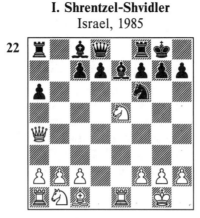

Black to play

8 ♔xh2 ♗b4! winning the queen or forcing mate; 8 ♘d5 ♖xc2, or 8 ♘e4 ♗c5+!! intending ♕h4. **Black wins.**

This is one occasion when it can be said that "a lone soldier (... or perhaps a lone rook) won the whole battle".

III. The pawns defending the king play the role of attackers

Karpov-Portisch
Turin, 1982

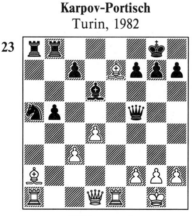

White to play

The battle up to now has been quite serene and no stormy events are expected. The two kings are both well protected, and White's next move is therefore all the more surprising. **1 g4!!**

The weakening of his king's position by the then world champion caused a sensation amongst the spectators. The pawn move, although dubious in positional terms, is tactically correct. By forcing the retreat of the black queen, White gains the upper hand.

1 ... ♛d7 This isn't the best move, but even after 1 ... ♛f4 2 ♗xd6 ♛xd6 3 ♛f3, or 2 ... cxd6 3 ♗d5, White still gains a considerable advantage. A possible continuation is 2 ♗xd6 ♛xd6 3 ♛f3 ♛d7 4 ♖e2 ♖a6 5 ♖ae1 ♖f6 6 ♛g3 with many threats.

2 ♗xf7+! ♚h8 After 2 ... ♚xf7 3 ♖xa5! ♖xa5 (3 ... ♗xe7 4 ♛f3+) 4 ♛b3+ ♚g6 5 ♖e6+, White develops a mating attack.

3 ♗xd6 ♛xf7 4 ♖e7 ♛f8 5 ♗c5

Karpov points out laconically in his analysis of the game, "White has a material and a positional advantage; the game is decided."[7]

5 ... ♛f4 6 ♛e2 h6 7 ♖e4 Black resigned after another 10 moves.

IV. The queen as a blockader

Parma-Portisch
Bled, 1961

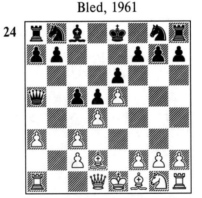

Black to play

1 ... ♛a4 The second move of the queen in the opening stage of the game. Still, it has an important goal: to put pressure on White's queenside pawns (c2, d4 and a3) whilst preventing the opponent from gaining space (in particular, foiling the move 2 a4). Play continued **2 ♛g4 g6 3 ♖c1 ♘c6 4 ♘f3 h6 5 ♗d3 c4 6 ♗e2 ♗d7 7 ♛f4 ♖h7! 8 h4 0-0-0** with a double-edged game.

The black queen neutralises White's chances on the queenside.

The next example is another illustration of the queen blockading the enemy position.

Timman-Geller
Linares, 1983

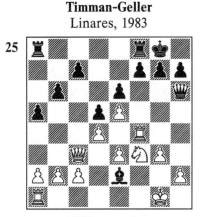

White to play

1 **♕c6!!** A full appreciation of the implications of this very strong move requires deep understanding. The queen prevents Black from gaining counterplay by the freeing moves ... c5 and ... f6. After 1 ... ♗xf3 2 ♖xf3 ♖ac8 3 ♖af1 it is difficult for Black to prevent the plan 4 c3, 5 ♕d7!, 6 ♖xf7!

1 ... **♕h5 2 ♔g2 ♖ae8 3 ♖e1 ♗a6** (3 ... ♗xf3+ was preferable) **4 g4 ♕g6 5 ♔h1 ♖e7 6 g5 ♕h5 7 ♔g2 ♖b8 8 ♔f2 ♕g6 9 ♖f6! ♕e4 10 ♖f4 ♕g6 11 ♖c1 ♖c8 12 ♖f6 ♕e4 13 g6!**

Winning immediately. 13 ... hxg6? 14 ♖f4 or 13 ... gxf6 14 exf6 ♖7e8 15 gxf7+ etc.

13 ... **♖f8 14 ♖f4 fxg6** Or 14 ... ♕xg6 15 ♖g1 ♕h5 16 ♖h4 ♕f5 17 ♖g5 and the queen is trapped.

15 **♖xe4 dxe4 16 ♕xe4 c5 17 c4 Black resigns.**

V. Placing a piece within the enemy's firing range

In the next two positions White deliberately posts one of his pieces in a position where it may soon come under attack. This can be likened to deliberately provoking the enemy — waving a red flag in front of a bull.

Keene-Ljubojevic
Moscow, 1977

White to play

Consider, for example, Keene's move **1 ♕f5!?** in diagram 26. The queen is placed on the diagonal of Black's queen's bishop and it's obvious that she will soon have to find a new spot.

That added pressure on Black's kingside is ample compensation for the loss of time is shown by the various possible continuations **1 ... d6 2 ♘xf6+ gxf6 3 ♕h5** or **1 ... ♗e7 2 ♘xe5 d6 3 ♘xc6 bxc6 4 ♘xe7+ ♕xe7 5 ♕f4;** in both cases White has a good position.

Keres-Kotov
Budapest, 1950

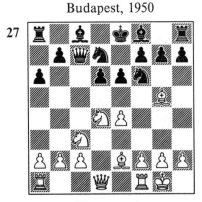

White to play

1 ♗h5 'invites' 1 ... g6 which significantly weakens the dark squares.

If 1 ... ♘e5 2 ♗xf6 gxf6 3 ♔h1 intending 4 f4. In this variation the bishop is strongly posted on h5. 1 ... ♘xh5 2 ♕xh5 g6 3 ♕h4 ♗g7 4 ♖ad1 is also more comfortable for White.

Meanwhile White is threatening 2 ♘xe6. The game continued 1 ... ♕c4? 2 ♘xe6!! Anyway! 2 ... ♕xe6 3 ♘d5! White develops a crushing attack. 3 ... ♔d8 4 ♗g4 ♕e5 5 f4 ♕xe4 6 ♗xd7 ♗xd7 7 ♘xf6 gxf6 8 ♗xf6+ ♔c7 9 ♗xh8 and **White won.**

VI. Placing a wedge between your opponent's pieces

Baker-Basman
London, 1978

28

Black to play

In this position, Black ignored the threat to his knight and played **1 ...♗a6!** The grovelling 2 ♗f1 was forced, still leaving the advantage with Black. But White decided to check the correctness of his opponent's idea.

2 cxb4 ♗xb4 3 ♘c3 ♘xc3 4 a3

Had Black miscalculated? Continuing 4 ... ♗a5 5 b4, or 4 ... ♘e4 5 ♕xb4, or 4 ... ♘d5 5 axb4 he loses material.

4 ... ♘b1!! This isn't a routine move but it is very effective. The black knight cuts the connection between the white pieces, allowing 5 ♕xb4 to be met by ♕xc1 mate.

5 axb4 ♘xd2 6 ♗xd2 ♕c4 and **White resigned** after several moves.

In diagram 29 the state of the black king seems precarious even though the squares g6, g7 and g8 are currently protected. White's next

Dzindzichashvili-Browne
New York, 1984

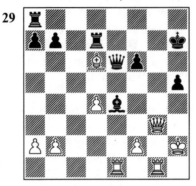

White to play

move prevents the rook at a8 participating in defensive operations:
1 ♗b8! ♕e8 White threatens 2 ♖xe4 ♕xe4 3 ♕g8+ with mate. **2 ♖xe4!**
♕xb8 Or 2 ... ♕xe4 3 ♕g8+ ♔h6 4 ♕h8+ and mates.

3 ♖e5! fxe5 4 ♕g6+ ♔h8 5 ♕h6+ Black resigns.

4
Flexibility

Chess experts advocate conceiving a plan in the early stages of the game and then carrying it out. This recommendation, although basically sound, is applied too rigorously by many chessplayers. There are those who will continue with their original plan, even though it is 'bankrupt', by refusing to think again, and possibly devise a new strategy taking account of the changed situation.

Willingness to change, and the connection between external events and our own internal world, are essential prerequisites of any creative discovery.

I. Giving up the trump card

G. Zakhodiakin
USSR, 1932

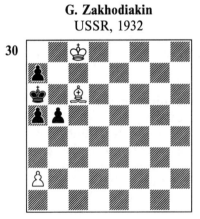

30

White to play and win

It is well known that a king and a bishop cannot mate a lone king. Therefore it would appear that White's chances of success rest solely on his ability to defend his a2-pawn. However, checking the possibilities reveals that Black can force the exchange of the last white

29

pawn by means of the manoeuvre 1 ... a4 and then ... ♔a5-b4-a3. White cannot defend the pawn by 1 a3 because of 1 ... a4 2 ♔c7 ♔a5 and ... b4. Further consideration reveals that, in fact, if White gives up the trump card, the a2-pawn, he can weave a mating net. **1 a4!! bxa4 2 ♔c7 a3 3 ♗a4!** 3 ♗d7? a4! and the black king escapes **3 ... a2 4 ♔c6 a1 = ♕ 5 ♗b5 mate!**

Szapiel-Keres
Poland, 1950

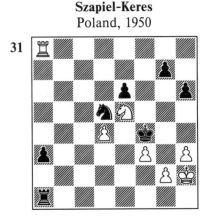

31

Black to play

During the adjournment of the game Szapiel-Keres, Black became convinced that the natural continuation 1 ... a2 would fail to bring victory after 2 ♖a3! E.g., 2 ... ♘c3 3 g3+! (3 ... ♔g5? 4 ♖a7) or 2 ... ♘e3 3 ♘d3+ ♔g5 4 ♘b4.

Finally he found a solution which at first glance seems quite absurd: to forfeit his outside passed pawn — which is only two squares away from promoting — in order to improve the positioning of his pieces.

1 ... ♔e3!! Keres' opponent reckoned that this was an oversight[8] and immediately replied **2 ♖xa3+ ♖xa3 3 ♘c4+ ♔f2 4 ♘xa3.** It was only after **4 ... ♘e3!** that he realised that he had no hope of salvation.

The game continued **5 f4** Or 5 g4 ♘f1+ 6 ♔h1 ♘g3+ 7 ♔h2 ♔xf3 8 ♘b5 ♘e2 and wins.

5 ... ♘xg2 6 f5 exf5 7 d5 ♘f4 8 d6 g5 White resigned several moves later. After 9 d7 g4 10 hxg4 fxg4 11 d8=♕ g3+ he is mated.

In the position shown in diagram 32, White enjoys a considerable advantage, mainly because of the weakness at c7 and the bad bishop at g7.

Sultan Khan-Flohr
Prague, 1931

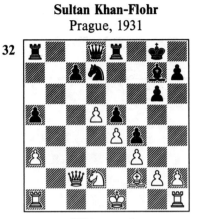

White to play

1 0-0 ♗f8 2 ♖fc1 ♗d6 3 ♘c4 ♕e7 4 ♘xd6!

Quite surprising. Within one move he allows Black to rid himself of the two major defects in his position ... Nevertheless, this is the correct move. White will now gain absolute control of the b- and c-files. The a5-pawn will eventually fall and the White a-pawn will promote without interruption.

4 ... cxd6 5 ♖ab1 ♘f8 5 ... ♖ec8 6 ♕xc8+ ♖xc8 7 ♖xc8+ ♔f7 8 ♖b7 is hopeless for Black.

6 ♕c6 ♖ab8 7 ♖b6! ♖xb6 8 ♕xb6 ♕d7 9 ♖c6 ♖c8 Trying to tempt White into 10 ♖xd6? ♖c1+ 11 ♗e1 ♖xe1+ 12 ♔f2 ♖b1!

10 ♗e1! Black resigns

Another example is shown in the next diagram where one side gives up what at first hand appears to be his strongest weapon.

Black is threatening 1 ... ♗e2 with the intention of leaving White without reasonable moves. Logic would suggest that a break-out on the queenside, thereby creating a passed pawn, would be White's only hope.

1 b5! cxb5 2 cxb5 axb5 3 a6 b4 4 a7 ♗e4 5 a8=♕!!

The obvious continuation 5 ♖b2 g3 6 ♖b3+ ♔f4, would lead to defeat (7 a8=♕? h2+!). But now, on sacrificing the source of his pride, the a-pawn, White could still manage to draw. **5 ... ♗xa8 6 ♖b2 g3 7 ♖b3+ ♔f4 8 ♖xb4+** Sacrificing the pawn has enabled White to play this move with check.

Sergievsky-Khasin
USSR, 1978

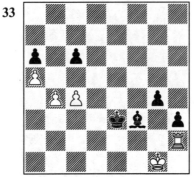

White to play

8 ... ♗e4 9 ♖b2 Draw

II. Change of direction

One of the characteristics of flexibility of thought is the ability to adopt different solutions to the same problem — being prepared to change direction, to abandon an idea that appeared promising but will in fact not bring the desired result, and to adjust quickly to the ever-changing situation on the board.

L. Olimutzky
USSR, 1963

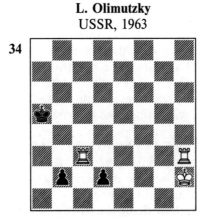

White to play and win

A glance at the diagram indicates that White will have to concentrate his efforts on stopping the black pawns from promoting.

The first moves which suggest themselves are **1 ♖a3+ ♔b4 2 ♖ab3+ ♔c4** Not 2 ... ♔a4? 3 ♖bg3! b1=♕ 4 ♖h4+ ♔b5 5 ♖g5+ leading to mate or the winning of the queen. **3 ♖hc3+ ♔d4 4 ♖d3+ ♔c4!** White has managed to place his rooks on the b- and d-files to prevent the pawns from promoting, but how should he continue? Black is threatening 5 ... b1=♕! 6 ♖xb1 ♔xd3 and 5 ... d1=♕! 6 ♖xd1 ♔xb3, with a draw. For White to win, he must come up with a new plan.

5 ♖bc3+ ♔b4 6 ♖c7!! b1=♕ 7 ♖d8!! d1=♕ 8 ♖b8+ ♔a3 9 ♖a7+ and **White wins** both new queens and the game.

In the last position the notion of change of direction involved a change in idea. White, in order to reach his goal, changed from plan A (capturing the black pawns) to plan B (a mating attack). In the following two diagrams the 'change in direction' occurred literally as well as metaphorically.

In pawn endings, material advantage is nearly always the deciding factor. However, here is an ending in which, on the premise that the closed position does not allow a breakthrough, a draw was agreed even though White has a two pawn advantage.

Brugeman-Daryus
Botzov, 1969

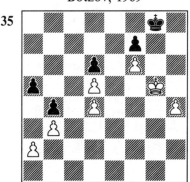

35

White to play

Any attempt by the white king to reach the a5-pawn will be countered by the black king moving towards the white pawn at f6. Note that if a race were to occur, the *black* king would reach his target first.

Despite all this there is still a win to be gained.

1 ♔f5 ♔h7 2 ♔e4 ♔g6 3 ♔d3 ♔xf6 4 ♔e4!!

The king gives up his journey to the queenside and returns to his place on the king's flank!

It transpires that the loss of the pawn at f6 creates a path for the white king and White wins.

4 ... ♔g6 5 ♔f4! f6 Or 5 ... ♔f6 6 h5 **6 h5+** and **White wins.**

If, at the third move, Black avoids capturing the f-pawn, White can move to the queen's flank: 3 ... ♔f5 4 ♔c4 ♔xf6 5 ♔b5, and again White wins.

Karpov-Taimanov
Leningrad, 1977

36

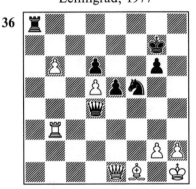

Black to play

White appears to have a promising position in that he has an extra passed pawn on the b-file.

However, White's last move (1 b5-b6?) allowed Black a beautiful combination. **1 ... ♖a1 2 ♖b1 2 ♕e2 ♕xd5 3 ♖b5 ♘d4!** is no better. **2 ... ♘g3+!! White resigns!** 3 ♕xg3 ♖xb1 wins 'simply' and 3 hxg3 is met by returning the rook to base − 3 ... ♖a8!! − when mate is unavoidable.

III. Conducting operations in several parts of the board.

At a certain period of time, a chess struggle is usually fought in a small part of the board, on a limited number of squares. It is uncommon to implement a plan that extends over a very large (chess) space. The following diagrams show the exception.

Barcza-Tibor
Debrecen, 1931

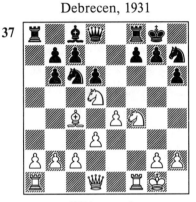

White to play

1 ♘g6!

An obvious sacrifice that cannot be accepted: 1 ... fxg6?? 2 ♘e7++ ♚h8 3 ♘xg6 mate.

1 ... ♖e8 2 ♖xf7! ♚xf7

At the cost of a whole rook White has destroyed the black king's defences. However, attempting to activate the battery ♗c4/♘d5 does not bring the desired result. Hence ...

3 ♕h5!! The death blow comes from an unexpected direction. Escape routes are closed; 3 ... ♚g8? 4 ♘de7 mate! **3 ... ♗e6 4 ♘ge7+ ♚f8 5 ♖f1+ ♘f6 6 ♖xf6+ gxf6 7 ♕xh6+ ♚f7 8 ♕xf6 mate.**

In diagram 38, **1 ... ♕xb2!** A spirited sacrifice. Not 1 ... ♘f2+ 2 ♖xf2 ♕xf2 3 ♗xf6 ♗xf6 4 ♘e4 and White wins.

2 ♘a4 ♘f2+!! 3 ♖xf2 ♘e4!!

This is the tactical blow that was prepared by Black in advance. White can no longer avoid material losses.

4 ♖f1 ♘g3+ 5 ♚g1 ♕xa1 6 ♕xa1 ♗xa1 7 ♖xa1 ♘xe2+ 8 ♚f2 ♗xe6! 9 ♖e1 c3 10 ♖xe2 ♖ac8 11 ♘d4

Kouatly-Murey
Paris, 1988

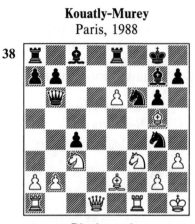

Black to play

Also insufficient is 11 ♖c2 b5!
11 ... ♗d7 White resigns

A. Maksimovskikh
USSR, 1976

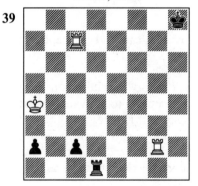

White to play and draw

This seemingly simple position demands exact play on White's part, which extends to the whole board.

1 ♖c8+ ♔h7 2 ♖c7+ ♔h6 3 ♖c6+ ♔h5 4 ♖c5+ ♔h4 5 ♖c4+ ♔h3 6 ♖c3+ ♖d3!

With the intention of driving off the white rook from the c-file. Not 6 ... ♔xg2? 7 ♖xc2+ and 8 ♖xa2 =. But now, after 7 ♖xd3+ ♔xg2,

White is utterly lost.

7 ♖h2+! ♔g3 8 ♖g2+ ♔f3 9 ♖f2+ ♔e3 10 ♖e2+ ♔d4

Black's king was forced to leave the third rank, but now the other white rook comes into play again.

11 ♖c4+! ♔d5 12 ♖c5+ etc. **Draw**

IV. Borrowing ideas from the opponent

During the chess battle a player tends to draw his ideas from within, basing them on his knowledge, experience and the tossing and turning in his own mind. Here is another source of ideas — the opponent! Appreciating the opponent's ideas affords us a glimpse inside his mind, and allows us at a later stage to use it as a very effective weapon for our own purposes.

Positions such as these are usually *symmetrical* positions.

J. Dorogov
1st prize, Shakhmaty v SSSR, 1976

White to play and win

In this study by Dorogov, White wins as follows: **1 g6 b2 2 ♘c3!**
2 ♔c2? d3+ 2 ... dxc3 3 ♔c2

The black pawns are stopped temporarily, and now Black has to handle the white pawns.

3 ... ♔e7 4 g7 ♘f6 5 exf6+ ♔f7 6 h5 ♔g8 7 h6 a3 8 ♔b1 c6 9 f3 c5 10 f4 c4 11 f5

Has Black run out of moves?

11 ... c2+ 12 ♔xc2 b1=♕+ 13 ♔xb1 c3

And now is White in *zugzwang?*

14 f7+! The symmetrical position allows him to use the same trick. **14 ...** &xf7 **15 g8=**&+ &xg8 **16 f6**

A mutual *zugzwang*. Black loses because it is his turn to move and so he must allow the promotion of one of the white pawns.

Vilenev Esclapon
1910

41

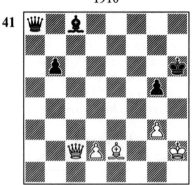

Whoever moves — wins!

In the piquant position in diagram 41, the side to move wins by using the same idea. If White is to move first:

1 &h5! Threatening &g6 mate.

1 ... &xh5 **2** &h7+ &g4 **3** &h3+ &f3 **4** &g2+ winning the queen.

If Black is to move first: **1 ...** &h3! **2** &xh3 &h1+ **3** &g4 &h5+ **4** &f5 &g6+ and wins.

5
Goal orientated thinking

The Soviet grandmaster Alexander Kotov once described the following incident.[9] A group of masters were analysing an endgame and couldn't decide which way to play to secure victory. The former world champion, Capablanca, entered the room, glanced at the board and within seconds moved all the pieces until a certain configuration was reached which guaranteed victory.

Capablanca didn't make a few isolated moves but rather created a new scheme. This type of thinking is reminiscent of Gestalt theory[10] according to which the *whole* is the first unit to be examined and not the parts. A person has to learn a task as a complete entity, and not as a collection of separate components.

The thought process developed in the present chapter is characterised by raising the question, "where should pieces be in order to achieve the aim?", without taking into consideration the limitations imposed by the current position. Such thinking focuses on the final objective and directs the means (the pieces) for the actualisation of this goal.

Benko-Bilek
Budapest, 1957

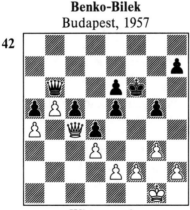

White to play

I. Improving the position of a single piece

The position shown in diagram 42 seems balanced in that the advance of White's passed pawn down the b-file is blocked by the black queen. Grandmaster Benko creates a winning plan based on the far-sighted manoeuvring of his queen.

1 ♕c1! White is preparing to offer a queen exchange to liberate his passed pawn. This can be best achieved on a6, and 1 ♕c1! is the first step towards this square.

1 ... h6 2 h4 ♕d6 3 hxg5+ hxg5 4 ♕b1 ♕b6 Otherwise 5 b6 **5 ♕f1 e4** A desperate attempt at counterplay. On other moves the manoeuvre ♕g2-a8-a6 is decisive.

6 ♕h3 ♕d8 7 ♕h6+ ♔e5 8 ♕g7+ ♔d6 9 dxe4 g4 10 ♕b7 ♕c7 11 e5+ ♔d7 12 ♕xc7+ ♔xc7 13 ♔f1 c4 14 ♔e1 ♔b6 15 ♔d2 ♔c5 16 f3 and **Black resigns**

Tal-Shagalovich
USSR, 1955

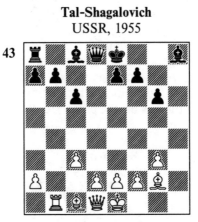

43

Black to play

In the Tal-Shagalovich game, Black realised that the exchange of rooks on the h-file has temporarily weakened the position of both kings. This inspired him with the idea of penetrating with his queen to White's first rank: **1 ... ♕a5! 2 ♕b3 ♕h5**

Black has brought his queen to the kingside using the diversionary attack on the a2-pawn. White made a mistake and played **3 ♗f3?**

Later analysis proved that the move **3 ♔f1!** would have saved White's game. The continuation 3 ... ♕h2 4 e4 ♗h3 5 ♗xh3 ♕h1+

6 ♔e2 ♕xe4+ 7 ♔d1 ♕h1+ 8 ♔c2 ♕xh3 9 ♕xb7 ♕f5+ 10 ♔b2 ♕c8 would have kept a positional and material balance.

3 ... ♕h2 **4 e4 g5!** Threatening 5 ... ♕g1+ 6 ♔e2 g4. It is interesting to see how Black develops a strong attack within the space of a few moves. White can't find a satisfactory defence and loses quickly.

5 d3 ♕g1+ 6 ♔e2 g4 7 ♗g5 gxf3+ 8 ♔xf3 ♕h2 9 ♗h4 ♗f6 10 ♗xf6 ♕h5+ 11 ♔f4 or 11 ♔g2 ♗h3+ intending 12 ... ♕f3. **11 ... ♕h6+ 12 ♗g5 e5+ 13 ♔f3 ♕h5+ 14 ♔e3 ♕xg5+ White resigns.**

II. Improving the position of several pieces

Latonov-Krasenkov
USSR, 1985

44

Black to play

In this position White is not in a good state, but then neither is Black's win easy. Neither 1... ♕d1 2 ♔f1, nor 1 ... ♕e5!? 2 ♗e3 forces a decisive result.

For Black to win, *the positions of both the black queen and rook need to be changed* such that the rook will be at the head of the battery in front of the queen. Once the goal has been determined the path to victory isn't complicated.

1 ... ♕a4! **2** ♗d2 Black threatened 2 ... ♖d1 and the defence 2 b3 fails to 2 ... ♕a5!

2 ... ♖d6! **3** ♔f1 There is no satisfactory defence against 3 ... ♕d7 **3 ...** ♕b5+ **White resigns.** He would have suffered heavy material losses after 4 ♕e2 (or 4 ♔g1 ♕d7) 4 ... ♕xb2 5 ♗d3 ♕d4.

III. Devising a scheme that involves the co-ordination of the whole set-up

T. Petrosian-Taimanov
USSR (ch), 1955

45

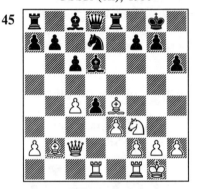

White to play

Black has just captured the white d4 pawn. We would normally expect a routine recapture, but instead White finds a surprising continuation **1 ♗h7+! ♔h8 2 ♖xd4 ♗c5**

Analysis shows that after 2 ... ♕e7 3 ♖e4 ♕f8 4 ♖h4 ♘e5 5 ♘g5! White also has a strong attacking position.

3 ♖f4 The check on the first move has enabled the rook to take up a threatening position against the black king.

3 ... ♕e7 4 ♖e4! ♕f8 5 ♖h4 An original manoeuvre of the rook. The immediate threat is 6 ♖xh6.

5 ... f6 6 ♗g6 ♖e7 7 ♖h5 Vacating the h4-square for the white knight, thereby taking advantage of the weak light squares.

7 ... ♗d6 8 ♖d1 ♗e5 9 ♗a3! c5 10 ♘h4 Black resigns

Possible continuations were 10 ... ♕d8 11 ♗xc5, or 10 ... ♕g8 11 ♗h7! ♕xh7 12 ♘g6+ with decisive material gain. The white pieces worked together in perfect harmony.

In diagram 46, Black has a good position and by playing the standard, 1 ... gxf5, he would restore material balance and thereby keep his advantage. All the black pieces, apart from the rook on a8, are in good, strong, influential positions. The question is whether or not he can direct his entire army in a combined attack against one common

Cnaa'n-Kalir
Israel (ch), 1969

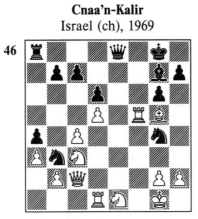

Black to play

target. Black finds a convincing answer.

1 ... ♗d4+! 2 ♔h1 Forced. 2 ... gxf5 3 ♘d3 He had to take urgent measures against the threat 3 ... ♘f2+.

3 ... ♗e3! 4 ♗h4 ♘d4 5 ♕b1 ♕h5 Black's now fully co-ordinated forces are generating tremendous power and each move creates a new threat.

6 ♗g3 ♘xh2! 7 ♗xh2 ♘f3! and **White resigns**

Bastrikov-Ragozin
USSR, 1942

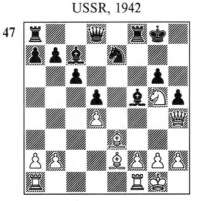

Black to play

Black's play in this position is a superb example of thinking based on holistic, comprehensive concepts. Ragozin doesn't just organise his pieces in a casual way, rather he creates a mental picture of what position his pieces should be in and only then begins to manoeuvre them to the desired posts.

1 ... ♕d6! 2 g4 At first glance, this appears to seize the advantage for White (2 ... hxg4?? 3 ♕h7 mate). **2 ... ♕f6!**

His queen takes up a strong position, and incidentally prevents 3 gxf5? because of 3 ... ♘xf5 4 ♕h3 ♘xe3 5 ♕xe3 ♖ae8 6 ♕d2 ♗f4 and wins.

3 f4 ♖ae8 4 h3 ♘c8 5 ♕f2 ♗b6! 6 ♖ad1 Capturing the bishop still isn't possible: 6 gxf5? ♖xe3!

6 ... ♘d6 Within a few moves all of Black's pieces are in key positions.

7 ♗f3 ♗d7 8 a4 ♔g7 9 b3 ♖h8 10 ♔g2 hxg4 11 hxg4 ♘f7 12 ♘xf7 ♕xf7 13 ♖h1 ♗c7!

Once again Black positions his pieces in a new formation, even more effective than the previous one.

This time the pressure is focused on the h2-b8 diagonal.

14 ♕d2 ♕e7! 15 ♗f2 ♕d6! 16 ♗e3 g5! Winning both material and the game. **17 ♖xh8 ♖xh8 18 ♖h1 gxf4** and **Black won.**

Ravinsky-Smyslov
USSR (ch), 1944

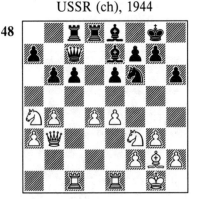

Black to play

White appears to be in a solid and stable position. True, the f2-square is slightly weak, being only protected by the king, but since no black pieces have crossed the *third* rank, White cannot perceive any danger.

1 ... c5! 2 dxc5 ♗xa4 3 ♕xa4 bxc5 4 ♗f1 ♕b6 5 b5 c4! The weakness of the f2-square begins to show. The continuation 6 ♗xc4 ♘g4 gives Black some dangerous threats.

6 h3 c3 7 ♕b3 ♗c5 8 ♖c2 ♖d2! 9 ♖xd2 cxd2 10 ♖e2 ♗xf2+! 11 ♔g2 ♖c3! 12 ♕d1 ♗e3 13 ♘xd2 ♕d4 14 ♕e1 ♘xe4

Looking back to the position in the diagram, we can only marvel at the wealth of imagination and the depth of vision shown by Smyslov. The dramatic change that has taken place is demonstrated by the dominating positions of the black pieces — a sharp contrast to White's helplessness. The game concluded: **15 ♘xe4 ♕xe4+ 16 ♔h2 ♕d4 17 ♖g2 ♖c1 18 ♕e2 ♕a1 19 ♕xe3 ♖xf1 20 g4 ♖e1** and **White resigns.**

Bondarevsky-Botvinnik
USSR (ch), 1940

49

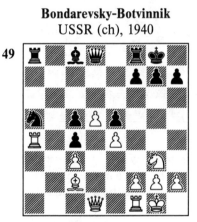

White to play

The weakness of the doubled and isolated Black c-pawns is clear. Temporarily the knight on a5 is also placed awkwardly. However, it is not easy to exploit this.

What is needed here is not a short-term plan asking, "what should be the next move?", but rather an integrated build up of White's whole force.

1 ♕h5! f6 2 ♖fa1 ♗d7 3 ♖4a3 ♕b6 4 ♕d1!

The queen has completed its duties on the kingside. By gaining a tempo (the threat on e5) the way has been cleared for the doubling of rooks on the a-file. Now the queen returns to increase the pressure.

4 ... ♖a7 5 ♘f1 ♖fa8 6 ♘e3 ♔f8 7 ♖1a2 ♖a6 8 h3

White is in no hurry. The pawn on c4 is doomed and Black also has to take account of the unpleasant threat 9 ♖xa5 ♖xa5 10 ♘xc4.

8 ... ♕d8 9 ♘xc4 ♗b5 10 ♘xa5 ♖xa5 11 ♕a1 ♖xa3 12 ♖xa3 ♖xa3 13 ♕xa3 White has a winning advantage. 13 ... ♕c7 14 ♕a8+ ♔f7 15 ♗d1 ♔g6 16 ♗g4 ♗d7 17 d6! ♕xd6 18 ♕d8 ♕d2 19 ♕xd7 ♕e1+ 20 ♔h2 **Black resigns.**

Goldin-Efimov
USSR, 1982

White to play

In the battle that follows, White plays a series of impressive moves. That withstanding, the first move in the series, simple and obvious as it may appear, is the strongest and the most important move in the whole game.

1 a4!! Allowing the rook to join the attack and to become the decisive factor. **1 ... ♘d6**

Unfortunately he couldn't reply 1 ... a6? 2 axb5 axb5 3 ♖xa8 ♕xa8 4 ♗xf6.

2 axb5 ♘xb5 3 ♖a6! ♗xg5 4 ♘xg5 ♕xd5 5 ♖h6!

Threatening 6 ♖h8+! followed by 7 ♕h5+ and mate. The rook cannot be taken – 5 ... gxh6? 6 ♘e6+.

5 ... ♕d3 6 ♘h7 f5 7 ♕g6 ♕d2 attacking both rooks, but White has a crushing response. **7 ♕e6+ ♖f7 7 ... ♔h8? 8 ♘g5+. 8 ♕e8+! ♖f8! 9 ♘f6+** and **Black resigns**, since he is mated.

It is worthwhile pointing out again that 1 a4!! is the decisive move; all the later hammer blows stemmed from this modest beginning.

Kasparov-Smirin
USSR (ch), 1988

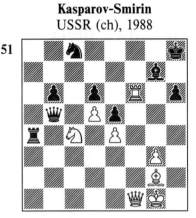

White to play

White seems to have a promising attacking position, but his pieces are 'hanging' and a convincing breakthrough is not easy to find. Neither 1 ♗h3 ♖a1! nor 1 ♖f8+ ♗xf8 2 ♕xf8+ ♔h7 guarantee success.

1 ♖e6!! Making way for the queen. If 1 ... ♖xc4? 2 ♕f7 with a decisive attack.

1 ... ♔g8 2 ♗h3! ♖xc4 3 ♖xh6!! Now he uses the rook to clear a path for the bishop. After 3 ... ♕c5+ 4 ♔h1 ♖c1 the white queen is pinned, but its power is sufficient to force mate − 5 ♗e6 mate.

3 ... ♗xh6 4 ♗e6+ ♔h8 5 ♕f6+ Black resigns

Since if 5 ... ♔h7 (5 ... ♗g7? 6 ♕h4+) 6 ♕f7+ ♗g7 7 ♗f5+ ♔h8 8 ♕h5+ ♔g8 9 ♗e6+ ♔f8 10 ♕f7 mate.

6
Removal of your own piece

The *enemy* piece that foils our plans is an everyday occurrence on the chessboard. However, the same can't be said of the player's own pieces. The chessplayer is not very often preoccupied with the question, "How do I get rid of one of my own pieces?"

The diagrams in this chapter contain positions wherein one of the sides, to achieve his objective, had to remove one of his own pieces. As we will see in diagram 52, this is not always a very easy task.

V. Vlasenko
2nd Prize, Chervony Girnik, 1983

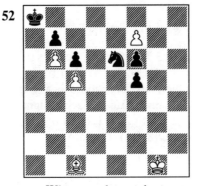

White to play and win

1 ♗f4!
The continuation 1 ♗h6 followed by 2 f8=♕ does not win, as the black king will stay on the squares a8 and b8 and any attempt to come near it would only create stalemate.

1 ... ♘d8! Not 1 ... ♘f8? 2 ♗d6 ♘e6 3 ♔f2 when White wins.

2 f8 = ♘! Naturally, 2 f8 = ♕(♖)? is stalemate. With the text White retains an extra piece, but is now forced to counter some heroic 'suicide-attempts' by his opponent.

48

2 ... ♘e6! 3 ♘g6 ♘f8 4 ♘h4 ♘g6 5 ♘g2 ♘h4 6 ♘e3 ♘g2!

The final touch. The continuation 7 ♗h6 ♘xe3 8 ♗xe3 f4 is only a draw, for reasons described in the first note. White, however, saves the last word for himself:

7 ♘d5! **White wins.**

I. Removal of your own piece to achieve stalemate

The most widespread application of the removal of one's own piece(s) is in seeking to bring about a stalemate. In the following position, White's material inferiority, along with the 'delicate' positioning of his king, suggests that all his energies should be directed towards the creation of this.

Sliwa-Doda
Poland (ch), 1967

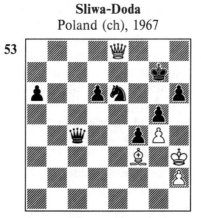

53

White to play

1 ♕e7+! ♔g6 Or 1 ... ♔g8 2 ♕e8+ ♘f8 3 ♗d5+! ♕xd5 4 ♕xf8+! ♔xf8 stalemate. 2 ♗e4+! ♕xe4 3 ♕g7+ ♔xg7 **stalemate!**

Two symmetrical variations (echo): one could say that this is a composed study 'hidden' in a real game.

Pachman's study (diagram 54) is more difficult to solve. From a material point of view, White's position is excellent, but the threats 1 ... ♕c3+ and 1 ... ♔b3+ give Black the upper hand. Also 1 ♕c2+ ♔b4+! costs White his queen. Salvation is found in the total sacrifice of all his pieces in order to force a stalemate.

V. Pachman
1st Prize, *The Problemist*, 1980-81

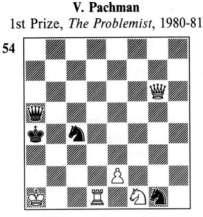

White to play and draw

1 ♖d2!! ♔b3+ The move 1 ... ♕c3+ has lost its force since the b2-square is now protected. **2 ♔b1 ♘a3+ 3 ♔c1 ♕c3+ 4 ♕c2+!! ♘xc2 5 ♖d3! ♘xe2+ 6 ♔d1 ♕xd3+ 7 ♘d2+ Draw!** Every retreat of the king allows White a stalemate, while the continuation 7 ... ♕xd2+ 8 ♔xd2 results in king and two knights versus king which is a theoretical draw.

In the next position we will witness a very creative way (some may say *too* creative) of removing one's own piece.

Shtern-Kushnitzky
"Spartak" (ch), 1952

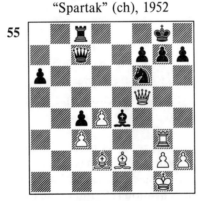

White to play

When a composer of studies or problems wants to change a position, it is easy; after all, he created the position. The pieces are simply shifted by a rank or a file.

Things are a lot more difficult for the competitive chess player who has to operate within the limitations of a given position and according to the strict rules of the game. On that note, the following incident is amusing.

White played **1 ♖xg7+!** (not 1 ♕xf6 ♕xg3!) **1 ... ♔xg7 2 ♗h6+! ♔xh6 3 ♕xf6+ ♗g6 4 g4 ♕a5 5 h4**

Isn't it time to resign? The player of the black pieces obviously didn't think so. He removed the a6-pawn from the board (!) and played **5 ... ♖c5!! 6 dxc5 ♕xc5+ 7 ♔f1 ♕g1+! A stalemate!**

After he had finished his little joke, Black, of course, confessed and resigned accordingly.

II. Removal of your own piece to prevent stalemate

This is in effect the reverse of the theme discussed in the previous section. In this instance we have to give up a piece in order to *prevent* our opponent from creating a stalemate position.

Capablanca-Em. Lasker
Berlin, 1914

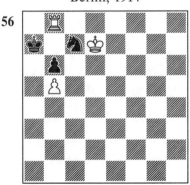

White to play

This is an imaginary position which is based on a rapid game that was played between these two former world champions.

1 ♔xc7 puts Black into a stalemate position, while putting the rook anywhere along the eighth rank is met by 1 ... ♘xb5 with a simple draw.

It is interesting that the very *existence* of the rook is ruining White's chances of winning. Therefore **1 ♖a8+!! ♘xa8** 1 ... ♔xa8 2 ♔xc7 or 1 ... ♔b7 2 ♖a7+! leads to the same position **2 ♔c8** Aiming at a theoretically winning position − 2 ... ♘c7 3 ♔xc7 ♔a8 4 ♔xb6 and so on. **White wins.**

III. Removal of your own pieces for different purposes

Apart from stalemate, there are other reasons to justify the removal of one's own piece. The position in the next diagram gives expression to the theme of *clearing a square.* In the subsequent diagram White gets rid of his knight *to maintain the characteristics* of the position. In diagram 59, removal of one's own piece gives rise to *the opening of a diagonal* and the next position gives an example of *path clearance.*

S. Kozlowski
Swiat Szachowy, 1931

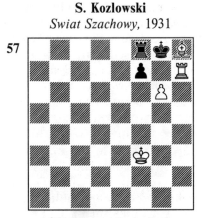

White to play and win

In this position the obvious continuation 1 g7 ♖a8 is a draw; the extra white bishop remains imprisoned and his material advantage is not capitalised on. In order to win, White must achieve the same position without his useless bishop.

1 ♖g7+ ♔xh8 2 ♖h7+ ♔g8. The objective has been achieved and the win comes quickly. **3 g7!**

Every move of the black rook allows 4 ♖h8+, a move which previously had been impossible as long as the white bishop occupied the square h8.

Y. Afek
2nd commendation, Themes - 64, 1978

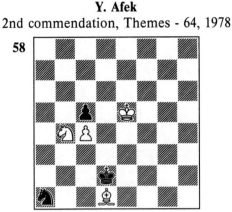

White to play and win

White's material advantage is only temporary in Afek's study, in that White is about to lose one of his pieces. The draw seems inevitable: 1 ♗a4? cxb4 2 c5 b3 3 ♗xb3 ♘xb3 4 c6 ♘a5, and Black will stop the pawn.

1 ♘c2 ♘b3 Obviously not 1 ... ♘xc2 2 ♗xc2 ♚xc2 3 ♚d5 and wins. **2 ♘a1!!**

Fantastic! The obvious move, 2 ♘e3, fails because of 2 ... ♘a5! 3 ♚e4 ♘xc4! drawing. After the knight's astonishing move Black is forced to capture it since the alternative 2 ... ♘a5 loses to 3 ♘b3+!

2 ... ♘xa1 Take another look at the diagram − the position is identical to that occuring two moves later but with a single exception: White has got rid of his knight. The change in the positions of the pawns has been avoided (cxb4 is impossible) and this factor enables White to win. **3 ♗a4 ♚c3 4 ♚d5 ♚b4 5 ♗d1**

Black is in *zugzwang* and every move he can make loses. In effect, White is a piece up − the black knight is neutralised at the edge of the board with no hope of rescue: 5 ... ♘b3? 6 ♗xb3 ♚xb3 7 ♚xc5.

5 ... ♚a5 6 ♚xc5 and **White wins.**

In order to solve the study in diagram 59, think of the children's game, 'What happens if'? What would happen without the white rook? Answer: White would win with the move 1 d4 mate.

Is it possible to get rid of the white rook quickly without giving Black enough time to organise a defence? Yes, it is!

L. Kubbel
1917

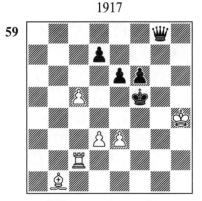

White to play and win

1 ♖f2+ ♔e5 2 ♖f5+!! ♔xf5 Or 2 ... exf5 3 d4+ ♔e6 4 ♗a2+ d5 5 cxd6+! e.p. and wins.

3 d4 mate!

From a study by H. Steniczka
Schach Echo, 1965

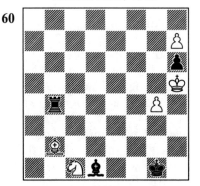

White to play and win

In diagram 60 the obvious continuation, 1 h8=♕, will lead to the loss of the queen after 1 ... ♖xg4!, in that 2 ♗d4+ ♔f1! does not help. Due to the discovered check by the rook, the queen is lost no matter which move she makes.

In addition, neither are 2 ♔xh6 ♖h4+ nor 2 ♗g7!? ♖f4+! 3 ♔g6

♗c2+! 4 ♔h5 ♗d1+ with a draw, any good.

Let us imagine that the white bishop is no longer on the board. Will there be any significant changes? Will there be any fresh possibilities previously not open to White?

1 ♗d4+!! ♖xd4 2 h8=♕ ♖xg4 3 ♕a1!!

The purpose of White's first move, initially incomprehensible, now becomes apparent. The sacrifice of the bishop cleared the way to a1 for the queen. **3 ... ♖a4+ 4 ♘e2+!** and **White wins.**

IV. Turning a hindering piece into a helping one

If it is not possible to remove a hindering piece itself from the board, sometimes it can be transformed from a liability to a helpful and supporting piece.

In diagram 61, White would have been happy if the bishop on f8 could have been made 'to disappear', thus allowing mate (♖d8+). However, through lack of choice, he cleverly turns the 'hindrance' to great use.

On the surface it appears that White can mate on g7 or on the back rank. A closer look reveals that Black has strong counter threats against the white king. For example, 1 ♖d8? ♗f2+! and, paradoxically, it is Black who wins.

Bertrina-Ghitescu
1974

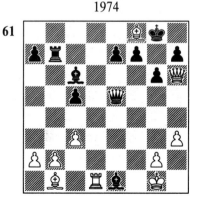

61

White to play

1 ♗g7!! Not only does he block the mating square g7, but he is willing to sacrifice his rook as well!

1 ... ♗f2+! 2 ♔f1! 2 ♔xf2? ♖xb2+ 2 ... ♗b5+ Not 2 ... ♗xg2+
3 ♔xf2! ♖xb2+ 4 ♔g1! but 2 ... f6 was better. 3 ♔xf2 ♕e2+ 4 ♔g3 ♕xd1
5 ♗h8!!

All that, obviously, White should have foreseen. White threatens
6 ♕g7 mate, and if 5 ... ♔xh8, then 6 ♕f8 mate.

Black resigns. 5 ... ♕d6+ 6 ♔f2 only delays the end.

K. Feyter
1938

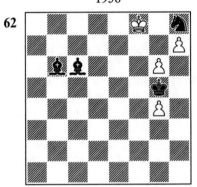

62

White to play and draw

In diagram 62, the position that closes this chapter, White can
choose between two possibilites in promoting a pawn. One possibility
will turn the promoted piece into a *hindering* piece, whilst the second,
which he in fact chose, promotes it into a *helping* piece.

1 g7 ♗c5+ 2 ♔g8 ♗d4! 3 gxh8=♘! 3 gxh8=♕? ♗d5+ and Black
wins.

3 ... ♗d5+ 4 ♘f7+ ♔g6 5 h8=♘+! Again, 5 h8=♕? ♗xf7+ and wins.
Draw

7
Reducing the importance of the time element

The notion of time in chess (tempo) is central to the way of thinking and planning of chess players. The term 'tempo' refers to many different factors crucial to the playing of a game, including the relative speed of pieces' entrances into battle in the opening stage, the rate of a passed pawn against the opponent's attempts to stop it, etc.[11] Posing a threat which forces the opponent to defend himself gives us *time* to carry out our plans. Alternatively, giving the opponent free rein to choose his moves is likely to give him the necessary time to get organised and foil our plans. This is the reason why the chess attack, apart from being *powerful*, must conform to the criterion of *speedy execution*.

The following positions are peculiar as they demonstrate players' total disregard of the time element. It transpires that some plans are so powerful that their slowness does not detract from their success.

Many players are reluctant to devise, never mind implement, a time-consuming plan on the assumption that it is being unrealistic, and they therefore overlook many promising and interesting lines of action.

In diagram 63, White stunned his opponent with **1 ♘d2!!**
Such a move demanded accurate and careful calculation. At first glance White's chances of success look slim. **1 ... ♘xd2 2 a5** 2 ♔xb6 h4 and Black wins. **2 ... bxa5** Actually, Black resigned at this point. The continuation 2 ... ♘c4 3 a6 ♘d6 4 ♔xb6 h4 5 ♔c5 h3 6 a7 ♘b7+ 7 ♔b4 h2 8 a8=♕ h1=♕ 9 ♕h8+ also leads to defeat.

3 b6 ♘c4 4 b7 ♘e5 If not for the pawn a5, Black would win immediately by means of 4 ... ♘a5! Even now what can White do? 5 b8=♕? ♘c6+ loses.

5 ♔b8!! The only move to win. Despite the process of queening taking a long time, it is inevitable. For example, 5 ... ♘d3/d7+ 6 ♔c8!, or 5 ... ♘f7/c4 6 ♔c7! **White wins**

Szabo-Groszpeter
Hungary, 1984

63

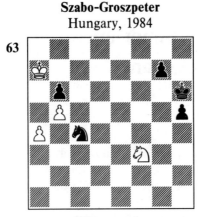

White to play

Verner-Donchenko
Moscow, 1979

64

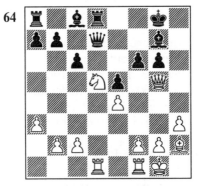

White to play

Verner-Donchenko continued **1 ♘xf6+ ♗xf6 2 ♕xf6 ♕xd1! 3 ♗xe5 ♕d7**

Up to here it was easy to understand. White has sacrificed his rook for a strong attack and, if he wants, he can force a perpetual check (♕h8+ − f6+ − h8+). Can he, however, achieve more than that?

4 ♔h2!! Wonderful. The threat is 5 ♖d1. The move could not have been played though, without the previous preparatory move as the rook would have been captured with **check**.

Now Black no longer has a defence: even with his material advantage and the right to move he cannot prevent the fall – 4 ... ♖e8 5 ♕h8+ ♔f7 6 ♕g7+ ♔e6 7 ♕f6 mate, or 4 ... ♖f8 5 ♕xg6+, or 4 ... ♕f7 5 ♕h8 mate, or 4 ... ♕h7 5 ♕xd8+ **Black resigns**

Beilin-Lipnitsky
USSR, 1951

65

Black to play

Black is ahead in development, but any delay will allow White to save himself by 2 g3, 3 ♗g2 and 4 0-0.

1 ... e3!! 2 ♕xd7 ♖ac8 The sacrifice of the bishop was designed solely to prevent White from freeing himself. Black's attack develops slowly but with great power. **3 ♕a4**

On 3 ♕b5 ♖xc3 4 ♕b2 ♖fc8 5 ♖xc3 ♖xc3 6 g3, 6 ... ♖b3!! wins for Black.

3 ... ♖xc3 4 ♖d1 ♖fc8 5 g3 ♖c1 6 ♗h3 White completes his development and threatens to castle while remaining with a decisive material advantage. **6 ... ♖xd1+ 7 ♕xd1 ♕c3+ 8 ♔f1 ♕d2!** With the idea of 9 ♕xd2 exd2 10 ♔f2 ♖c1 winning.

9 ♔g2 Has White been saved?

9 ... ♖c1! White resigns. Neither 10 ♕xd2 exd2, nor 10 ♕xc1 ♕xe2+ give him any reason to continue.

With his last move (in diagram 66), Black attacked the white bishop on b2. Apparently he expected either 1 ♗c1 or 1 ♕c7 ♕xb2 2 ♕xc8+ ♔g7, keeping a comfortable position in each case. However, there was a surprise in store for him ...

Keres-Malich
Varna, 1962

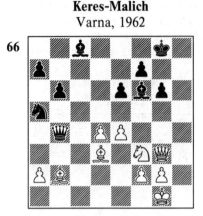

White to play

1 ♕c7 ♕xb2 2 e5!!

Creating a strong attack with minimal forces. Black can't defend himself even though he is a piece up and has the move. For example: 2... ♗g7 3 ♕xc8+ ♗f8 4 ♗xg6! fxg6 5 ♕xe6+ with a crushing attack (6 ♘h4, or ♘g5 according to Black's reply).

2 ... ♗e7 3 ♕xe7 ♕c1+ 4 ♗f1!

Not 4 ♔h2 ♕f4+ 5 ♔h3 ♗b7 after which Black manages to defend himself.

4 ... ♗b7

4 ... ♗a6 loses to 5 ♕d8+ ♔g7 6 ♕f6+, followed by ♘g5.

5 ♘g5 ♕f4 6 g3 and **Black resigns** without waiting for 6 ... ♕f5 7 ♗d3.

Evaluating the position from Lurya and Mitrofanov is, so it seems, a simple matter. The white bishop has to stop the black a-pawn from promoting. Right? Anyway, if both sides are to promote, White must make sure that he does so first. True? And if neither of the above occur, than the whole proceedings will result in a draw, won't they?

No, no, no! **1 ♗e4!** The bishop isn't intending to stop the black pawn ... ! **1 ...** ♔f6 1 ... a2 2 h7 a1=♕ 3 h8=♕+ and wins. **2 ♗e8! a2 3 ♔f8! a1=♕** White is *not* the first to promote ...

4 h7 And the position *isn't a draw* ...

White wins. Black can't stop, at one and the same time, the mate and the capture of his queen. White's first move prevented the reply 4 ... ♕a8+.

From a study by Lurya & Mitrofanov
USSR, 1983

67

White to play and win

Hamann-Velimirovic
Harrachov, 1967

68

Black to play

From the position in the diagram, Black continued **1 ... ♘xg2!
2 ♗xg2 f4** On the surface of things, there isn't anything particularly exciting or interesting. Black has temporarily sacrificed a piece which he will win back immediately. But in actual fact, Black has absolutely no intention of capturing the white bishop. Rather, his aim in sacrificing the knight was to clear the way for an onslaught of the black pawns and pieces.

3 ♘f1 a6 4 a4 b6 5 h3 ♕f7! 6 ♕f3 ♖a7 7 ♗h2 h5 8 ♘d2 g4 9 ♕d1 ♕f6

10 a5 ♕h4 11 hxg4 hxg4 12 axb6 ♖af7 13 ♕c2 ♗h6 14 ♖eb1 ♗g5

Slowly, slowly, as if he has all the time in the world, Black masses his pieces in preparation for a decisive attack. All this whilst being a piece down and having a white pawn two squares away from queening!

15 ♕d3 f3 16 ♗g3 ♕h5 17 ♘f1 fxg2 18 ♔xg2 ♕h3+ 19 ♔g1 ♖xf2!
White resigns

Tal-Bilek
Miskolc, 1963

69

White to play

1 ♕g3! a4 2 ♖xf6! ♖xf6 3 ♕xe5 axb3 4 axb3!!

Being a rook down does not induce White to hurry. Black is unable to use the time he is given to free himself.

4 ... b6 On 4 ... ♔f7 5 ♘xf6 ♕xf6 6 ♕c7+ White wins. The text move prepares to reply to 5 ♖f1 with 5 ... ♖a5, with some chance to hold the endgame. However, White does not give his opponent any hope.

5 b4! Black resigns.

8
Alertness to Subtle Differences

Many instances in life, and also in chess, appear to confirm that 'all roads lead to Rome'. However, closer scrutiny often reveals that only one path is correct and the others — even though very similar — will lead us astray.

The smallest of details are often of the greatest importance, and minute changes in a position can often change a losing position into a winning one, and vice versa.

I. Static identity versus dynamic identity

Is it possible that exactly the same position can, on separate occasions, have different possibilities for the same players?

N. Petrovic
Problem, 1960, 1st Prize

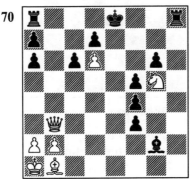

Mate in 8 moves

An attempt to create a direct mating attack, in this problem by Petrovic, will fail because Black keeps open the option of castling. For example 1 ♕c3 0-0! or 1 ♗d3? ♖h1+ 2 ♗b1 0-0-0!

The prevention of these defences is the rationale behind the following moves.

1 ♕b7 ♖d8 1 ... 0-0? **2 ♕xd7 2 ♕b3 ♖a8** As a defence against 3 ♕f7 mate. **3 ♗d3 ♖h1+** White threatened 4 ♕f7+ ♔d8 5 ♕f6+ ♔c8 6 ♗xa6+ ♔b8 7 ♕xh8 mate.

4 ♗b1 ♖h8

We have returned to the position in the diagram, but with one crucial difference: Black can no longer castle since his rooks have already moved. Hence the two positions are *the same*, but they are not *identical*.

5 ♕c3 ♖h7 Or 5 ... ♖f8 6 ♕g7. Now **6 ♕f6** is followed by **7 ♘xh7** and **8 ♕e7 mate**

In the following diagram we will examine the same position moved one rank upwards, a factor which has significance because of the symmetrical characteristics of the chess board.

Y. Hoch
1st Prize, Mandil Memorial tournament 1980

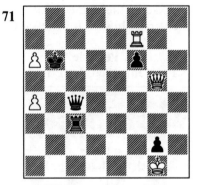

71

White to play and win

It is tempting in this position to play 1 ♖xf6+ ♔a7 2 ♕g7+ which wins the black queen. However the continuation 2 ... ♕c7 3 ♖f7 ♖c1+ 4 ♔xg2 ♖c2+ 5 ♔f3 ♖c3+ 6 ♔e4 ♖c4+ 7 ♔d5 ♖c5+ 8 ♔e6 ♖c6+ 9 ♔f5 ♖c5+ 10 ♔g6 ♖c6+ 11 ♔h7 leads only to a draw after 11 ... ♔xa6! (12 ♖xc7 ♖xc7 13 ♕xc7 stalemate!)

The solution is as follows **1 a5+!! ♔xa6 2 ♖xf6+ ♔a7 3 ♕g7+ ♕c7 4 ♖f7 ♖c1+ 5 ♔xg2 ♖c2+ 6 ♔f3 ♖c3+ 7 ♔e4 ♖c4+ 8 ♔d5 8 ♔f5? ♖f4+ 8 ... ♖c5+ 9 ♔e6 ♖c6+ 10 ♔f5 ♖c5+ 11 ♔g6 ♖c6+ 12 ♔h7 ♔a8!**

At first glance it appears that this variation will also end up drawn, as we saw before, but *there is* a difference **13 ♕g8+ ♕c8 14 ♖f8 ♖c7+ 15 ♔h8 ♔a7!** Inviting White to continue 16 ♖xc8 ♖xc8 17 ♕xc8 stalemate! A draw therefore?

16 ♕g1+ No! Since the whole picture in comparison to the first variation has been moved 'up' one rank, there now exists the possibility of checking along the a7-g1 diagonal, an option which was not previously available. **White wins.**

II. A minor change in the placing of the pieces

N. Elkies
3rd honourable mention, Czerniak Memorial, 1987

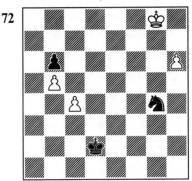

White to play and win

The striking simplicity of the position in diagram 72 is misleading. In fact the utmost accuracy is required here from both sides.

It is possible to predict with certainty that the black knight will be sacrificed for the white h-pawn. The black king will then move quickly over to the remaining pawns. White will play c4-c5 in an attempt to promote one of his pawns. A race will develop, in which White will promote when Black's c-pawn reaches the seventh rank. The result seems to be a theoretical draw.

Let's try: **1 ♔g7 ♘xh6 2 ♔xh6 ♔e3 3 c5 bxc5 4 b6 c4 5 b7 c3 6 b8=♕ c2 7 ♔g5 ♔d2!** (not 7 ... c1=♕?? 8 ♕f4+). Indeed, a draw.

White, though, has another possibility on the first move. **1 h7 ♘f6+ 2 ♔g7 ♘xh7 3 ♔xh7 ♔e3 4 c5 bxc5 5 b6 c4 6 b7 c3 7 b8=♕ c2** We have reached the same position but instead of the white king being on h6 it is now on h7. It takes a really overflowing dose of imagination to grasp from the diagram position the significance of the difference: **8 ♕h2!! c1=♕ 9 ♕h6+ and wins.** Note that 8 ... ♚d3 9 ♕h6 ♚e2 10 ♕c1 leads to the same result.

From a study by V. Neidze
5th mention, Havel MT, 1960

73

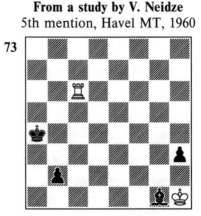

White to play and draw

A quick glance at the position in the diagram shows that it is not possible to stop the b2-pawn. White's only chance lies in trying to create stalemate possibilities. 1 ♖c1 is the natural choice (1 ... bxc1=♕/♖? stalemate!) but the move 1 ... bxc1 = ♘! (1 ... bxc1=♗? 2 ♚xg1 ♗f4 3 ♚h1 leads to a theoretical draw) frustrates it − 2 ♚xg1 ♘e2+ 3 ♚h2 ♘f4 4 ♚g3 ♚b4 and wins.

Conclusion: the move 1 ♖c1 leads to defeat.

Is it possible to take advantage of the idea of a stalemate in a different way?

1 ♖a6+! ♚b5 2 ♖a1! Draw. After 2 ... bxa1=♘ 3 ♚xg1 ♘c2 4 ♚h2 the black knight does not get to defend the h3-pawn in time.

In the Gutman-Vitolins game White sacrificed a rook and bishop in return for a strong attack. In diagram 74 he could now have crowned his attack with 1 ♕h6+! ♚g8 2 ♚d2 and 3 ♖g1+ but he transposed the moves by **1 ♚d2?** Threatening 2 ♖g1, or 2 ♕h6+ ♚g8 3 ♖g1+ ♚f7 4 ♖g7+ ♚e8 5 ♕h5+ and mate. 1 ... ♕e7 allows 2 ♕h6+ ♚g8 (2 ... ♕h7 3 ♕xf8+) 3 ♖g1+ ♚f7 and 4 ♕g6 mate. Is Black lost?

1 ... ♗d3!! 2 ♚xd3 Not 2 ♕h6+ ♗h7 or 2 ♕xd3 ♕e7 which allows Black to defend himself successfully. **2 ... ♕e7!**

Gutman-Vitolins
Latvia (ch), 1979

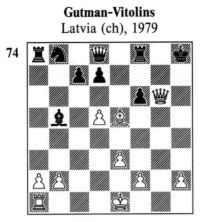

74

White to play

The purpose of the bishop sacrifice now becomes clear. On 3 ♕h6+ Black can defend himself by means of 3 ... ♕h7 *check*! **3 e4 ♕g7 4 ♕h5+ ♔g8** White's attack is repelled, and Black's material advantage guarantees victory.

5 ♗d4 c5 6 ♗xc5 ♖c8 7 f4 ♘a6 8 ♗f2 ♘b4+ 9 ♔e2 ♖xa2 White resigns.

From a study by J. Vandiest
4th commendation, de Feyter Jubilee, 1981

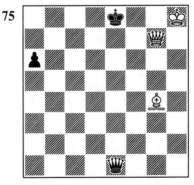

75

White to play and win

1 ♔g8 ♕e7 The only defence against the twin threats of 2 ♕f8 mate and 2 ♕d7 mate.

2 ♕g6+ ♔d8 3 ♕b6+ ♕c7 Forced 3 ... ♔e8? 4 ♕c6+ leads to immediate mate.

4 ♕e6!! *zugzwang*. Every move of the black queen will lose instantly. Pushing the a–pawn is the only possibility left for Black.

4 ... a5 5 ♕f6+ ♕e7 6 ♕b6+ ♕c7 7 ♕e6! Again. **7 ... a4 8 ♕f6+ ♕e7 9 ♕b6+ ♕c7 10 ♕e6!** And again. **10 ... a3 11 ♕f6+ ♕e7 12 ♕d4+!!** Now! **12 ... ♔c7 13 ♕a7+ ♔d6** 13 ... ♔d8? 14 ♕b8 mate. **14 ♕xa3+!** Winning the queen and the game.

III. The importance of move order

Ravinsky-Ilivitsky
USSR (ch, ½ final) 1952

White to play

The Averbakh-Bronstein game from the 1951, USSR Championship reached the position in diagram 76. The weak 1 g3? was answered firmly by 1 ... ♗xg5 2 ♕xg5 f6! (3 ♕xg7+ ♕xg7 4 ♘xg7 ♗h3!).

In his notes to the game, Grandmaster Lilienthal wrote that the storming sacrifices 1 ♘xg7 ♔xg7 2 ♕h6+ ♔g8 3 ♖xf4 exf4 4 e5 would not succeed because of 4 ... f5 (but not 4 ... ♘xd3? 5 ♗f6! and wins).

A year passed and Ravinsky deliberately entered into the position in a game against Ilivitsky. He played **1 ♘xg7 ♔xg7** 1 ... ♘cxd3? **2 ♕g3!** **2 ♖xf4 exf4 3 ♕h6+ ♔g8** Now, though, he changed the order of the moves, and instead of playing the incorrect 4 e5, preferred **4 ♗f6!! ♗xf6 5 e5**

There followed **5 ... ♘xd3 6 exf6 ♘f2+ 7 ♔g1 ♘h3+ 8 ♔f1 ♗c4+ 9 ♘e2 ♗xe2+ 10 ♔e1,** and **Black resigned.**

Demina-Rozenfeld
USSR, 1985

Black to play

Here Black could have won by 1 ... d1=♛+! and now, 2 ♛xd1 ♖e4+, or 2 ♖xd1 ♛b4+ 3 ♔g5 (3 ♖d4 ♖e4+) ♖xg3+! 4 ♖xg3 ♛h4 mate.

Instead, Black chose to play the combination with a different move-order. **1 ... ♖e4+?? 2 ♖xe4 d1=♛+ 3 ♖ge2!!**

A rude awakening. Suddenly it is *White* who wins.

IV. The importance of whose move it is

From a study by V. Pachman
1st Prize *Schachove Umeni,* 1980

White to play and win

In Pachman's study, a tempting continuation is 1 ♗g1+ ♔b8

2 ♗xh2+, but after 2 ... ♔b7! a position is reached such that, whatever move White makes, either the bishop or the rook is lost. Due to this seemingly inevitable loss of material, the game will apparently end in a draw.

However the careful reader will observe that White will win in the final position if it can be reached when it is *Black's* turn to move. Therefore: **1 ♗f2+!! ♔b8** 1 ... ♔b7 2 ♖a7+ and 3 ♖h7. **2 ♗g3+ ♔b7** 2 ... ♔c8 3 ♖a8+. **3 ♗xh2** In this position of mutual *zugzwang,* any move that Black makes ruins the controlling position of his pieces, and then White, once freed, will win using his material advantage.

9
Continuing calculation in a state of certainty

One of the most difficult dilemmas facing a chess player is when to stop calculating a series of moves.

Theoretically one can go calculating on and on, but there are clearly limits to it. The human brain is simply unable to carry on exact calculations of all the alternatives beyond a limited number of moves (even the world champions cannot forecast the end of play from the first moves).

Moreover, a lengthy calculation, even if feasible, necessitates a massive investment of energy and considerable time (which is unavailable to the competitive chess player).

As a result, the chess player uses an approach designed to avoid unnecessary effort. He looks for the 'good enough' alternative (Simon[12]) rather than the best continuation or the absolute truth.

According to this economical method, the chess player stops his calculations if they produce a satisfactory result – obtaining material advantage, a mating attack or a draw, according to the position and the player's ambitions.

We shall see the shortcomings of this way of thinking in the following examples.

In all of them we have a situation which seemingly justified the making of a decision without any further effort of calculation. But it transpired not to be so ...

Creative thinking in chess is marked by the refusal to take for granted 'proof', 'evidence', 'facts' and all such things which people sometimes use to oppose investigation and scrutiny.

A creative chess player will doubt, question, mistrust, disbelieve and refuse to accept anything as a final and absolute truth.

I. Calculation concerning the winning of material

In diagram 79, in the better position, Black played an erroneous combination: **1 ... ♗a3? 2 bxa3 b2 3 ♖xc2 ♕d1+** Not 3 ... b1=♕+ 4 ♖c1

71

Creative Chess

which wins the new queen due to the threat of mate on the back rank.

Murey-Zapata
Amsterdam, 1986

Black to play

4 ♔h2 ♕xc2 Black has stopped calculating in this position on the assumption that there was no way that the b-pawn could be prevented from queening.

5 ♕e5! Surprise! After 5 ... h6 6 ♗d4! the b-pawn is stopped after all. **5 ... f6 6 ♕xe6+ ♔f8 7 ♗a5 b1=♕ 8 ♗b4+ ♕xb4 9 axb4 ♕xa4 10 ♕d6+** and **White won.**

Vaganian-Westerinen
Moscow, 1982

Black to play

In the Vaganian-Westerinen battle, White had just captured Black's c6-pawn. Instead of recapturing, Black replied **1 ... ♕a5?!** thinking he could take his time.

The idea was to meet 2 cxb7 ♖xc3 3 b8=♕+ with 2 ... ♖c8+! when Black emerges a piece up.

The Soviet grandmaster saw through Black's idea, however, and found an even more ingenious coup to refute it.

2 cxb7! ♖xc3

In actual fact Westerinen chose 2 ... ♖b8 but still lost.

3 ♕a4+!! This is the move that Black had overlooked.

3 ... ♕xa4 4 b8=♕+ ♔d7 5 ♗b5+ and **White wins.**

Ehlvest-Vaiser
USSR (ch, ½ final) 1984

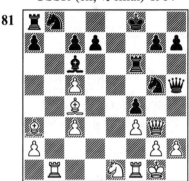

81

White to play

In this game between the two Soviet players, White played **1 ♕g4!**

Black is invited to play an ending which, after 1 ... ♕xg4 2 fxg4 ♗e4 3 ♖d1, is good for White in view of Black's undeveloped queenside. Vaiser reckoned that he could frustrate White's last move by **1 ... ♘xf3+2 gxf3 ♖g6**

White saw further ...

3 ♘g2!! ♖xg4 4 fxg4 and **Black resigns.**

He either loses his queen or is mated after 4 ... ♕h3 5 ♖xf4+ ♔e7 6 ♖e1+.

Also in the next position, one of the players calculated a variation which won the opponent's queen. However, it only became apparent after he pursued his plans that the queen was not such a good bargain.

Spielmann-Eliskases
Match, 1932

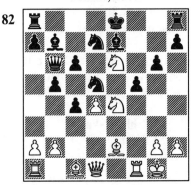

White to play

White had already sacrificed two of his pawns in order to achieve a dangerous attacking position, and he continues in daring fashion **1 a4!?** A direct attempt with 1 ♖xf5?!, hoping for 1 ... gxf5 2 ♗h5 mate, would have failed against 1 ... c5! **1 ... fxe4! 2 a5 ♕a6 3 ♕c2 ♘7f6 4 ♖xf6!**

Very nice. On 4 ... ♘xf6? 5 ♘c7+, and if 4 ... ♗xf6 5 ♕xe4 and the loss of the queen cannot be prevented. But *elegant* chess is not always *productive*. Black foresaw that the loss of his queen does not mean the end of the game.

4 ... ♗xf6! 5 ♕xe4 ♔f7! 6 ♘c5 ♖ae8 7 ♕f3 ♖xe2! Well, White has won the queen but he is losing the battle. 8 ♕xe2 releases the bishop from custody and permits 8 ... ♗xd4+, winning for Black.

8 ♘xa6 ♖e1+ 9 ♔f2 ♖he8 10 ♘c5 ♗c8 11 b4 ♔g8 12 ♗b2 ♖1e3 13 ♕d1 c3 14 ♗c1 c2! 15 ♕xc2 ♖e2+ 16 ♕xe2 ♗xd4+ 17 ♗e3 ♖xe3 18 ♕f1 Or 18 ♕xe3 ♗xe3+ 18 ♔f3 ♘xb4 and wins.

18 ... ♖a3+ and White resigns.

In diagram 83, play continued **1 ... ♗f6!! 2 ♗g4?**

White grabs the opportunity to win the exchange, but in retrospect he would have done better with 2 ♗d3 or 2 ♗c1.

2 ... ♕c7 3 ♗xc8 ♖xc8

Huzman-De Firmian
Moscow, 1989

83

Black to play

So White has won material, only to find out that he is facing a vicious attack.

4 c3 4 ♗c1? ♘a3+! 5 bxa3 ♕c3 wins **4 ... ♘a3+ 5 ♔a1 ♕xc3! 6 ♗c1**
So far it was easy for Black to find strong moves, but now he has to show what his attack is really worth. Of course, a draw is guaranteed (6 ... ♘c2+ 7 ♔b1 ♘a3+ etc.), but can he win?

6 ... ♕c2!! An extraordinary idea. Black threatens nothing but White finds himself in complete *zugzwang,* every move loses material, e.g. 7 ♕f3 ♕b1 mate; 7 ♕d3? ♕xd3 8 ♖xd3 ♘c2+; 7 ♖d3 ♕xc1+. Pawn moves will not postpone the inevitable for long: 7 g4 ♔h8 8 ?

7 ♕xc2 ♘xc2+ 8 ♔b1 ♘xe1 9 ♖xe1 ♗e5 10 b3 f6 11 ♖d1 ♖c3 12 ♗b2 ♖g3 and **Black won.**

The events in the Lombard-Del Corral game (diagram 84) are exceptional even in a book in which the exceptional is the rule.

White sacrificed a piece to achieve a better attacking position **1 ♖h3+ ♔g7 2 ♕xg6+ ♔f8 3 ♕h6+ ♔e8 4 e6** It seems that Black's fate has been determined. White is threatening 5 ♕g6+! ♖xg6 (or 5 ... ♔f8 6 ♕f7 mate) 6 ♖h8+, and mate.

4 ... ♘xe6 5 dxe6 ♕a5 6 ♕g6+! ♔d8 7 ♕xg8+ ♔c7 And so Black has managed to escape from mate. Meanwhile White has gained a material advantage of a whole *rook.* Is there any point in Black continuing with the struggle?

The stunning reply is that not only does Black continue, he forces a

Lombard-Del Corral
1973

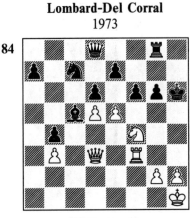

84

White to play

win! The white king is entrapped in a crushing attack.

**8 g3 ♕a1+ 9 ♔g2 ♕g1+ 10 ♔f3 ♕d1+ 11 ♔g2 ♕c2+ 12 ♔f3 f5!
13 ♘d5+ ♔b7 14 ♘e3 ♕e4+** and **White resigns.**

II. Calculation concerning the loss of material

Many chess players miss promising opportunities in their games because they do not seriously consider entering into positions where they are material down. In the romantic era of chess over 100 years or more ago, the game was played in a far less materialistic fashion than today. In the present era, most players will hesitate to sacrifice a pawn if they do not envisage real and speedy compensation for their investment.

From the position in diagram 85 the game continued **1 ... dxc3!
2 ♗xf7+?**

In retrospect, it would have been preferable to exchange queens and regain the piece (exf6). **2 ... ♔xf7!! 3 ♕xd8 cxb2** with a twin threat on the rook and the queen (4 ... ♗b4+).

4 ♕c7+ With this move virtually every chess player playing Black would have stopped, concluding that the variation was not worthwhile, resulting only in a material loss for Black. The West German player prepared a home-made bombshell: **4 ... ♔e6!!** A real knockout! All of a sudden it is blatantly obvious that the white queen has been lost on an open board and in broad daylight. After **5 ♗xb2 ♘a6,** or **5 ♕xc8+**

Larsen-Teschner
Wageningen, 1957

Black to play

♘8d7! 6 ♕xa8 bxa1=♕, White falls behind in material.
The game continued **5 ♕xc8+ ♘8d7 6 ♕xb7 bxa1=♕ 7 ♕xc6+ ♔f7**
and White is lost. From this hopeless position, incidentally, Larsen
succeeded in wresting a miraculous draw from his opponent.

Polyak-Levin
Kiev, 1949

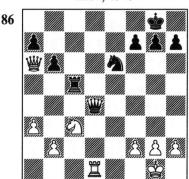

Black to play

1 ... ♖xc3!
Capturing the black rook or queen is obviously forbidden, and in
the meantime Black has won a piece. But it is not so simple ...
    2 ♕f1! Winning material, since Black cannot simultaneously defend

the queen *and* the rook.

2 ... ♖c8! 3 ♖xd4 ♘xd4

And so, White won the fight but he is losing the battle. The threat is 4 ... ♖c1! 5 ♕xc1 ♘e2+

4 ♔h1 Taking a step to avoid the knight fork but the queen cannot be saved. **4 ... ♘e2!** More aesthetic than 4 ... ♘b3. **White resigns.**

Fischer-Schweber
Buenos Aires, 1970

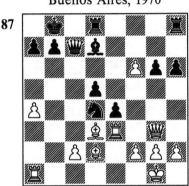

White to play

The above diagram is interesting in that the move played by White would be considered by almost all chess players, due to the simple win against any of Black's replies except *one*. The move will also be ruled out by almost every chess player because this reply looks to be a complete refutation of White's plan.

Former world champion Bobby Fischer continued to calculate one step further: **1 ♖xe4! ♕xg3** 1 ... dxe4?? 2 ♗f4 and wins, but what will White do now? 1 hxg3? dxe4 leaves black with a rook advantage.

2 ♖xd4!! It turns out that the black queen cannot escape as all its potential flight squares are covered by White's pieces. (The domination theme).

2 ... ♕g4 or 2 ... ♕c7 3 ♗f4. **3 ♖xg4 ♗xg4 4 ♗xg6** White has two pawns for the exchange and, besides, a strong passed pawn on f6. **White won.**

In diagram 88, Black played a surprising sacrifice: **1 ... ♘a4! 2 ♖xa4?** Much better is 2 ♕b4! Now White loses. **2 ... ♖d1+ 3 ♘e1 ♕d4!** Taking

Terentiev-Domuls
USSR, 1980

Black to play

advantage of the weakness of the first rank. **4 ♕e3!** The best defence. Not 4 ♕b4? c3. By means of the text move White is prepared to return material, and in actual fact, after 4 ...♕xe3 5 fxe3 ♖xe1+ 6 ♔f2, the danger of a loss has passed.

4 ... c3! 5 ♖a2 5 ♖xd4? exd4 6 ♕e2 c2 and wins. **5 ... ♕b4!** A quiet move that decides the battle. To play for so long with a material disadvantage, in the belief that his initiative would ultimately pay off, required great courage and a capacity for precise and extended calculation.

6 ♔f1 Or 6 ♖c2 ♕b1. **6 ... ♕xb5+ 7 ♕e2 ♖xe1+! 8 ♔xe1 ♕b1+ 9 ♕d1 ♕xa2 White resigns.**

There is a surprising and pleasurable finale to the study by Sadikov (diagram 89): **1 ♘g5!** 1 b7+? ♕xa5+ 2 ♖d2+ ♔c7 3 bxa8=♕ ♕xa8 4 ♖d7+ ♔xc6 5 ♖xe7 ♕a1+ 6 ♔e2 ♕b2+ and wins.

1 ... ♕xg5 2 ♖h8+ ♘g8 3 ♖xg8+ ♕xg8 4 b7+ ♔e7

Apparently all of White's efforts have been exhausted, but now lightning strikes from a clear sky.

5 ♗d8+!! ♕xd8 6 c7! and White with a king and two pawns forces a draw against a queen and a bishop!

A. Sadikov
USSR, 1968

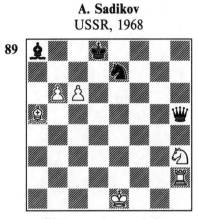

White to play and draw

III. Calculation of mate

There is no doubt that mate must be the concluding step of a calculated variation. Mate is a final position after which there is no need to calculate an opponent's counterplay. However, as we will now see, even here there is room for creative thinking.

Onescus-Gama
Rumania, 1956

White to play

Black has made a considerable material investment to reach this position, on the assumption that White cannot prevent mate. However, instead of resigning, White played **1 ♘xf3! exf3 2 ♕g7+!!**

Stunning. After 1 ... ♔xg7 the g-file is temporarily blocked, the g3 pawn is no longer pinned, and White continues 3 gxh4!

2 ... ♖xg7 3 ♖e8+ ♖g8 4 ♖xg8+ ♔xg8 5 gxh4 and White won.

Dunne-Plesset
New York State (ch), 1976

91

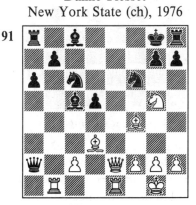

White to play

In the Dunne-Plesset game, White sacrificed a knight and gained in return a strong attack. He predicted an elegant way to finish the game:

1 ♕e8+?! ♘xe8 2 ♖xe8+ ♗f8 3 ♗d6 ♕xb1+ 4 ♗f1 g6 5 ♗xf8

Threatening 6 ♗h6 mate. The player of the white pieces, so proud of his glorious combination, went to call his friends to witness his achievement.[13] After 5 ... ♗d7 6 ♖xa8 there is no way to prevent mate.

Whether or not Plesset had foreseen the events in advance is merely academic. What is important is that he found the only move which prevents a defeat (and incidentally, *wins* the game).

5 ... ♕e1!! and White resigns.

There is no mate and White is left with a decisive material disadvantage.

And now for the end of the chapter, with a breath of optimism, a mate which is indeed ... a mate.

Can Black take the c2-pawn in diagram 92? 1 ... ♕xc2 will be answered brilliantly, 2 ♖e4!, and White wins (2 ... ♕xe4 3 ♕h6). But what about 1 ... ♖xc2? as played by Ivell?

Thipsay-Ivell
Great Britain (ch), 1985

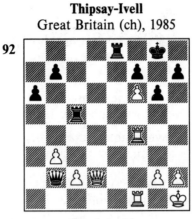

Black to play

He foresaw the continuation **1 ... ♖xc2 2 ♖e4!** and played the beautiful response **2 ... ♖ec8!** Now White cannot play 3 ♕h6? because of 3 ... ♕xf6! **3 ♖c4!!** The winning card. Black has no defence to the twin threats of 4 ♕h6 and 4 ♖xc8+ ♖xc8 5 ♕xb2 **3 ... ♕xf6 4 ♖xc8+ Black resigns.**

10
Violation of Theoretical Principles

Theoretical experts have established a set of principles and guide lines which are designed to instruct the chessplayer in his games.

Here is a random sample of such principles:

☆ Try to control the centre of the board.

☆ Castle during the early stages of the game.

☆ Don't waste time at the beginning of the game by moving the same piece several times.

☆ Don't make hasty pawn advances.

☆ Avoid exchanging while on attack.

☆ Try to avoid weakening the pawn formation protecting your king, and others ...

After witnessing one of the games of former world champion Tigran Petrosian, the English grandmaster Raymond Keene commented:[14] "it is possible to argue that the era of truly creative Western art has now passed and that all that remains for art to achieve is to parody former greatness ... if it is no longer possible to invent ideas that are truly original, than it is still possible, as an act of creative defiance to parody all the classical rules ..."

The following diagrams show a few situations where the chess player acted contrary to the accepted principles, rules and recommendations. This is not done as an act of protest or parody — as Keene reckons — but simply because in these specific positions the ordinary rules are invalid and one has to invent different rules.

I. Voluntarily entering into a pin

In diagram 93 Black played **1 ... f6!!**

After placing his king and his queen on the same file, he intentionally opens it ... offering an open invitation to the white rook, "come and take my queen!"

2 exf6 ♗c5+ 3 ♔h1 gxf6 4 ♖e1 0-0-0 5 ♖xe6 dxe6

White loses his bishop due to the threat of mate on the back rank.

Ljubojevic-Planinc
Vrsac, 1971

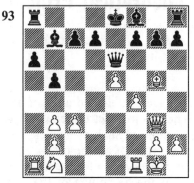

93

Black to play

6 ♕e1 fxg5 7 ♘d2 gxf4 8 ♕xe6+ ♔b8 9 ♘f3 ♖hg8
Black's strong initiative is more than adequate compensation for his insignificant material disadvantage.
   10 c4 b4 11 ♖f1 ♖g6 12 ♕f5 ♗e3 13 h3 ♖g3 14 ♕xh7 ♗xf3! 15 ♖xf3
15 gxf3? ♖d2 15 ... ♖d1+ 16 ♔h2 ♗g1+ 17 ♔h1 ♖g7! 18 ♕h8+ ♔b7
19 ♖d3 ♖e1 20 g3 Black threatened 20 ... ♗f2+ − g3+ **20 ... ♗d4+!**
21 ♔h2 ♖ge7!! White resigns.

Miles-Spassky
Montilla, 1978

94

White to play

1 ♘d7! with various threats: **2 ♘xf8, ♘xd5, ♘f6+.**

1 ... ♗c8

A little better would have been 1 ... ♗xc3 2 ♘f6+ ♔h8 3 bxc3 ♘e8, but White would still have kept the advantage.

2 ♘xd5 Naturally not 2 ♘f6+? ♕xf6! **2 ... ♔h8** Trying to take advantage of the ♘d7 pin. A grave mistake would have been 2 ... ♗xd7?? 3 ♕xd7 and White remains a pawn up.

3 ♘5f6 ♖a7

A third piece joins the attack. Other tries fail as well: 3 ... ♘e8 4 ♗e5, or 3 ... ♗e7 4 ♗e4.

4 d5! ♘e7 5 ♗e5! ♖xd7 5 ... ♗xd7? 6 ♕d4 and wins. After the text move, 6 ♕d4 is no longer on, because of 6 ... ♘c6!

6 h5! ♖xd5 7 ♕f4 ♖xd1 8 ♖xd1 ♕a5 9 ♘e8!

A beautiful finish. Avoiding mate is possible only at the cost of vast material losses: 9 ... ♖xe8 10 ♕f6 ♖g8 11 h6 ♘f5 12 ♗xf5 ♗f8 13 ♗xc8, etc.

9 ... f6 10 gxf6 ♔g8 11 ♘xg7 Black resigns.

Had Black played 10 ... ♖xe8, the game would have ended with the delightful 11 f7! ♖f8 12 h6 ♘f5 13 ♕xf5 ♗xf5 14 hxg7 mate.

II. Exchanging pieces when material down

From a study by V. Anufriev
2nd Prize *Shakhmaty Riga* 1979-80

White to play and draw

White's position in Anufriev's study looks hopeless. Besides being at a massive material disadvantage, he is also unable to leave the bishop protecting his pawn — the last remaining hope. (1 ♗f4? ♕d3, or

1 ♗g3 ♗b6 2 ♔h2 ♕d2 and wins). It's hard to believe that there exists a saving move, but reality in this instance supersedes the imagination. **1 ♗h2!!** He is even daring to offer an exchange of pieces!?

Black has two possibilities: to take on h2 or to pull back the bishop, so preventing a capture.

A   1 ... ♗xh2 2 ♗h3! ♕xh3 stalemate!

B   1 ... ♗b6 2 ♗h3! ♕xh3 stalemate!

In either position White has forced a *stalemate*. Only the piece on h2 changes its colour ... once black and once white ... a charming idea.

If in the previous diagram White's offer of piece exchanges was only to camouflage a stalemate-net, in the next diagram White sacrifices two pawns and is not perturbed by an exchange of queens initiated by Black.

Levenfish-Kan
USSR (ch), 1934

96

White to play

White played **1 ♘d6!**

Seemingly ignoring Black's next move **1 ... ♘xh3+,** White plays **2 ♔h2 ♘g5!** indirectly protecting the bishop. 3 ♘xb7 is met by 3 ... ♖xf3!

3 ♗g4 ♕xe5+ 4 ♖xe5 ♗a8 5 f4!

Another mysterious move that abandons a pawn, apparently without any compensation. It is interesting to note that some of the tournament participants thought that Levenfish simply didn't realise that his f-pawn was unprotected.

5 ... ♖xf4 6 ♗f5! The mist over White's idea begins to clear. In an ending with only a few pieces, and at a disadvantage of two pawns, he develops a decisive attack.

6 ... ♖xf5? loses immediately. But, even after the superior **6 ... g6!** **7 ♖e8+ ♔g7 8 ♖xa8 gxf5 9 ♖xa6**, White wins in the end, as is proved in a comprehensive analysis by Levenfish.[15].

7 ♘xf5 ♔f7 8 ♘d6+ and **Black resigns.** He also loses his bishop.

III. Intentional weakening of the pawn structure

Rotlevi-Nimzovitch
Karlsbad, 1911

97

White to play

From the position shown in the diagram, the battle continued **1 ♘e5! ♘cxe5 2 dxe5 ♘xe3 3 fxe3** Not 3 ♕xe3? d4. White intentionally forms tripled pawns on the e-file, an idea that would shock chess theoreticians, but in return Black's weak pawn on d5 is exposed to White's heavy pieces.

3 ... ♗b4 4 ♖ad1 ♕g5 5 ♗xd5 ♖d8 6 ♕c1 ♕xe5 7 ♗xe6 ♕xe6 8 ♖xd8+ ♔xd8 9 ♖d1+ ♔c8 10 ♘d5! Winning the c4-pawn and the game.

10 ... ♗a5 11 ♕xc4+ ♔b8 12 ♕f4+ ♔a8 13 ♕d4 f6 14 b4 ♗d8 15 ♖c1 and **White won.**

IV. Crazy castling

In diagram 98, as a result of sloppy play in the early stages, White is faced with considerable difficulties in protecting the pawns on his queen's wing. The continuations 1 ♗d2? ♗b2, 1 ♗xa3 ♕xc3+!, or 1 ♕d2 ♗xc1 all lead to the loss of a pawn.

Heidenfeld-Hecht
Nice (ol), 1974

98
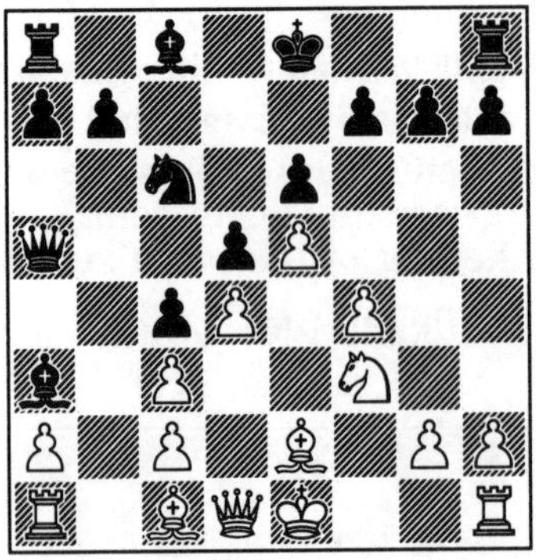

White to play

The next manoeuvre, completely irregular and strange as will be seen, is therefore essential. **1 ♔d2! ♗e7 2 ♕e1! ♗d7 3 ♔e3**

Now, whilst the queen defends the c3 pawn, the king can finish his trip over to a safe refuge.

3 ... f6 4 ♖f1 fxe5 5 fxe5 0-0 6 ♔f2 ♗e8 7 ♔g1

The trip is completed. 'Castling' was completed over five moves rather than one, but material equality was successfully maintained.

Ljubojevic-Seirawan
Tilburg, 1983

99
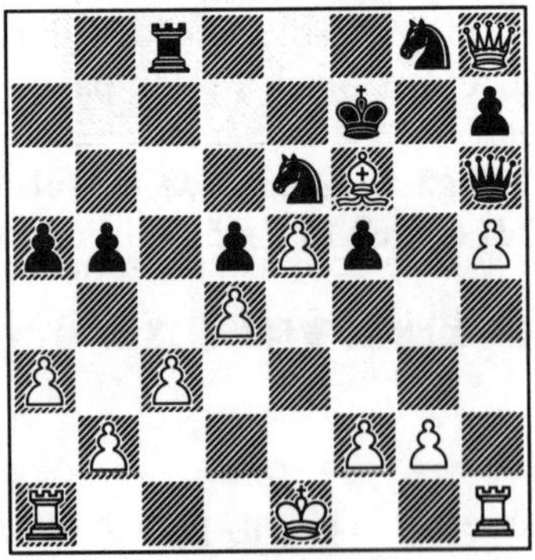

White to play

White is confronted with quite complex problems. In a chase for material conquests his queen got caught on the edge of the board, and is now threatened by 1 ... ♘e7. After 1 ♗h4 ♘g7 White is forced to turn back (2 ♗f6).

The Yugoslav Grandmaster finds a rare solution: **1 f4!! ♘xf4** 1 ... ♘e7? 2 ♗g5! **2 0-0! ♘e2+ 3 ♔f2 ♘f4 4 g4!**

Very original indeed. Firstly he castles and then immediately moves his king over to the centre before finally completely opening the pawn position protecting his king!

4 ... fxg4 4 ... ♘h3+ is met by 5 ♔g3! ♕e3+ 6 ♔h4! and wins. **5 ♗g5! ♕xg5 6 ♔g3 ♘f6** Or 6 ... ♔e6 7 ♖xf4 ♕xh5 8 ♖f6+! with advantage to White. **7 ♕xf6+ ♕xf6 8 exf6 ♘xh5+ 9 ♔xg4 ♘xf6+ 10 ♔f5** and **White won.**

V. Deserting a key-position

Botvinnik-Zuidema
Amsterdam, 1966

100

White to play

In this position the white rook is positioned behind the advanced c-pawn. That is its optimal position as recommended by theory. Surprisingly though, the rook must abandon this position in order to win the battle.

1 ♖e8!! Puts Black into *zugzwang*, e.g 1 ... c2 (1 ... ♗h8 2 g6+ ♔g7 3 ♖c8!) 2 g6+ ♔h6 3 ♖e2! c1=♕ 4 ♖h2 mate.

Black chose a different continuation in the actual game. **1 ... d3 2 g6+ ♔h6 3 ♖e3 ♗d4 4 ♖xd3 c2 5 ♖h3+ ♔g7 6 ♖h7+** and **Black resigns.**

After 6 ... ♔g8 7 ♖c7 the c-pawn falls and a theoretically winning position is reached — White wins by sacrificing his g-pawn and placing his king at g6.

IV. Weakening the king's defence

Ljubojevic-Larsen
London, 1980

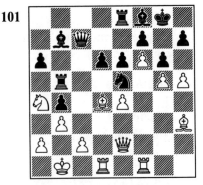

Black to play

White's situation looks safe. On the queenside his position is solid and any Black counterplay against the doubling of the white rooks on the h-file appears unlikely. Against this background, Black's next move seems all the more surprising. **1 ... gxh5!**

Voluntarily breaking up the chain of pawns defending his king. At this stage White cannot recapture a pawn in return (2 ♕xh5? ♗xe4), but in the long run Black's position doesn't inspire confidence. **2 ♗g2 ♘g4!** Threatening 3 ... ♖xg5 **3 ♕d2 ♕a5 4 ♖h1 h6!**

Not 4 ... ♖xg5? 5 e5! Only if White continues 5 ♖xh5 will 5 ... ♖xg5! come about; the manner in which Black defends his king's flank is very original. The very idea of standing up to an opponent in the place where at first sight he appears strongest is quite exceptional.

5 e5!? dxe5 6 ♗b6 ♖xb6 7 ♘xb6 ♕xb6 8 ♖xh5 ♗xg2 9 ♕xg2 ♘e3 10 ♕g1 ♘d5! 11 ♕xb6 ♘xb6 12 gxh6 ♘d5 13 ♖g1+ ♔h8! 13 ... ♔h7? 14 ♖g7+! **14 ♖xe5 ♘xf6** Black has repelled the attack and remained with a material advantage sufficient to win. After a few more moves, **White resigned.**

11
Absurd Moves

As can be understood from the title, this chapter is a collection of ideas which on the surface appear contrary to common sense. We are now about to remove the last layers of conformity!

I. Placing a piece in an unprotected position

J. Selman (version)

De Schakwereld, 1939

102

White to play and draw

White manages to achieve a draw by means of the stunning move **1 ♖e4!!**

What, in the name of God, is the meaning of this madness?

Black is forced to accept this sacrifice, but there is no concrete compensation for White in the offing: he is no closer to capturing the e2 pawn than he was before.

1 ... ♘xe4 2 ♘g6 Now if 2 ... e1=♕ (2 ... ♔b4 3 ♘f4 e1=♘ 4 ♔xa6 =) 3 ♘e5 – the sting. Black has to defend himself against 4 ♘c6 mate and by doing so he loses his queen. Without the sacrifice on the first move Black would have replied 3 ... ♕xe5. The e4-knight performs two negative functions: blocking the e-file and also the diagonal h1-a8.

2 ... ♘d6 3 ♘e5 ♘c8+ 4 ♔b7 ♘d6+ 5 ♔a7 ♘b5+ 6 ♔b7 Draw.

The difficulty in finding the first move was the need to place a piece on a square where it could be taken. In the next position the winning move entails putting a piece on a square where it can be taken in four different ways!

Penrose-Blau
Hastings, 1957-58

White to play

White wins by means of a short but very handsome trick: **1 e6! fxe6 2 ♘xd5!! ♘f5**

There is no better move, for example, 2 ... exd5? 3 ♖xe7+; 2 ... ♘xd5? 3 ♗xg6+; 2 ... cxd5? 3 ♗b5! and the worst of all, 2 ... ♕xd5? 3 ♕xe7 mate.

3 ♗xf5 Black resigns.

After 3 ... gxf5 4 ♖xe6+, the whole building collapses.

II. Placing a number of pieces in unprotected positions

Here boldness and imagination run completely wild — in view of the wide variety of opportunities available to the opponent. He can choose to capture which piece he wants and in what order.

In diagram 104, **1 e8=♕** Not 1 ♖h7+ ♔g1 2 e8=♕ ♗e5+ and Black wins. **1 ... ♗e5+ 2 ♕xe5!** The only move, e.g. 2 ♔g8 ♘h6+ 3 ♔f8 ♕c5+ 4 ♖e7 ♗d6; or 2 ♔h7 ♘f6+ 3 ♔g6 ♕g1+ etc.

2 ... ♕a8+ 3 ♖f8!! Pure chess magic.

3 ... ♛xf8+ **4** ♔h7 ♛f7+ **5** ♔h8 5 ♛g7? ♘f6+, with mate.

5 ... ♛f8+ **6** ♔h7 ♛h6+ **7** ♔g8 ♛g6+ **8** ♔h8 The white queen remains *en prise,* but instant stalemate would be the result of her capture.

8 ... ♛h6+ **9** ♔g8 and **draw.**

G. Nadareishvili
1st Prize, Mxedruly, 1975

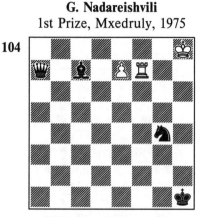

104

White to play and draw

Cordes–Miles
Bad Worishofen, 1985

105

White to play

In the Cordes-Miles game White played **1** ♗g5!!

Black, who with his last move attacked the white knight, certainly could not have anticipated this move, which places another white piece in a position where it can be taken.

1 ...　♖f8 Not 1 ... fxg5? 2 ♕e5+ ♔f7 3 ♘h6+, or 1 ... ♔f7 2 ♘h6+ ♔g7 3 ♘g4! fxg5 4 ♕e5+ ♔f7 5 ♘h6+. Of course, taking the knight was out of the question − 1 ... gxf5?? 2 ♗xf6, winning the queen.

2 ♕e5+! A third piece joins in with the circle of sacrifices! However, 2 ... fxe5?? would be inadvisable due to 3 ♘d6 mate. **2 ...　♔f7 3 ♘d6+ ♔g7 3 ♘xb7 ♘c6 4 ♕d5! ♕c7 5 ♘d6 fxg5 6 h4!** White has a decisive positional advantage. The continuation was **6 ... e3 7 f3 gxh4 8 ♖xh4 ♕d8 9 0-0-0 ♕e7 10 ♖dh1 ♖h8 11 ♘f5+! gxf5 12 ♕xf5 h5 13 ♖xh5 ♖xh5 14 ♖xh5 ♕e6 15 ♖g5+ ♔h8 16 ♕f4 ♕h6 17 ♖g8+ ♔xg8 18 ♕xh6,** and **Black resigned** after a few more moves.

III. A quiet move following a material sacrifice

The sacrifice of material is generally followed up vigorously either with a view to retrieving material, or to achieving an attacking objective. Situations in which a player with a material disadvantage makes a quiet move, without any real threat, are few and far between, even though the 'quiet move', in retrospect, turns out to be a very 'noisy' move which makes the opponent's defences fall apart.

Breyer-Esser
Budapest, 1917

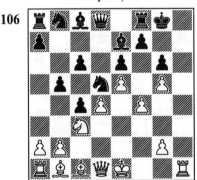

106

White to play

At an earlier stage of the game White sacrificed a knight in order to open up the h-file. The natural continuation in the diagram position is **1 ♕g4** with the idea of bringing the queen over to the h-file. In this event, after 1 ... ♔g7 Black has sufficient defensive resources. **1 ♔f1!**

At first glance this is a mysterious move which is quite difficult to fathom. **1 ... ♞xc3 2 bxc3 ♝b7 2 ... ♚g7 3 ♖h7+!**, with a similar continuation; but modern analysis showed that 2 ... ♛e8!, overprotecting g6, could have held.

3 ♛g4 ♚g7 4 ♖h7+! ♚xh7 5 ♛h5+ ♚g7 6 ♛h6+ ♚g8 7 ♝xg6 fxg6 8 ♛xg6+ ♚h8 9 ♛h6+ ♚g8 10 g6

If the white king was still at e1 then Black would have had a defence with 10 ... ♝h4+! and 11 ... ♛e7. White's first move prevented this and so left Black defenceless. **10 ... ♖f7 11 gxf7+ ♚xf7 12 ♛h5+ ♚g7 13 f5! exf5 14 ♝h6+**

With an additional piece joining the attack the end is nigh. After 14 ... ♚h7 the simplest way to win is by **15 ♝f4+ ♚g7 16 ♛h6+ ♚g8 17 ♛g6+ ♚h8 18 ♚e2**, with mate on the h-file.

A look at the following diagram gives the impression that Black's position is strong. He is threatening to mate at g2, and if, for example, 1 f3, then 1 ... g6 certainly leaves him solidly entrenched.

Polugayevsky-Khasin
USSR (ch), 1961

107

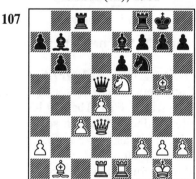

White to play

1 ♛h3!! This appears to be an elementary blunder when considering Black's following move.

1 ... ♖xc3 Winning a pawn (2 ♛xc3?? ♛xg2 mate) and also, with 'tempo', attacking the white queen!

2 f3 The devious trap that White has set springs into action: Black has no defence against the double threats of 3 ♝xf6 (and 4 ♛xh7 mate) and 3 ♗e4 gaining material.

The game continued: **2 ... h6 3 ♗xf6 ♗xf6 4 ♗e4 ♕xe4 5 ♖xe4 ♗xe4 6 ♘d7 ♗c2 7 ♘xf6+ gxf6 8 ♖c1 ♔g7 9 d5! exd5 10 ♕g4+ ♔h8 11 ♕d4** and **Black resigned** some moves later.

IV. Forcing the win by means of closing the position

Capablanca-Treybal
Karlsbad, 1929

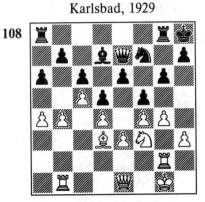

White to play

1 g5! Locking the king-side ... or maybe he intends to break through on the h-file?

1 ... ♕d8 2 h4 ♔g7 3 h5 ♖h8 4 ♖h2 ♕c7 5 ♕c3 ♕d8 6 ♔f2 ♕c7 Black is devoid of any counter chances, and has to wait patiently.

7 ♖bh1 ♖ag8 8 ♕a1 ♖b8 9 ♕a3 ♖bg8 10 b5! axb5 11 h6+ It appears that White has decided that his advantage on the left wing is enough for victory. With his last move he finally locks the king-side.

11 ... ♔f8 12 axb5 ♔e7 13 b6 Incredible. Instead of opening files, he systematically closes them. But meanwhile Black's scope for manoeuvre is narrowing.

13 ... ♕b8 14 ♖a1 ♖c8 15 ♕b4 ♖hd8 16 ♖a7 ♔f8 17 ♖h1 ♗e8 18 ♖ha1 ♔g8 19 ♖1a4 ♔f8 20 ♕a3 Slowly but surely White increases his preparations for the decisive action, in the only zone that's left unlocked.

20 ... ♔g8 21 ♔g3 ♗d7 22 ♔h4 ♔h8 23 ♕a1 ♔g8 24 ♔g3 ♔f8 25 ♔g2 ♗e8 26 ♘d2 ♗d7 27 ♘b3 ♖e8 28 ♘a5 ♘d8 29 ♗a6! A picturesque position. Black is helpless because his pieces have no space and he cannot bring aid to the weakness on b7. All this was achieved by White with his 'locking' moves.

29 ... bxa6 30 ♖xd7 ♖e7 Or 30 ... ♔g8 31 ♖g7+ ♔h8 32 ♖b4, with 33 b7, winning.

31 ♖xd8+ ♖xd8 32 ♘xc6 Black resigns.

V. Sacrificing material which is captured with check

In the next four diagrams White implements a rare idea: he sacrifices material, but not only does he not gain time to launch an attack, he even loses tempo since the sacrificed piece is captured with check!

V. Evreinov
1st Prize, *Shakhmaty Riga* 1959

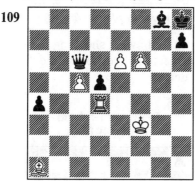

109

White to play and win

1 ♖e4!! At first this appears to be possibly the *worst* move that could have been played. It is, however, the only move that wins. It would have been no good to play 1 ♖d2 d4+, or 1 f7 ♗xf7 2 ♖g4+ d4+ 3 ♔f2 ♕xc5 4 ♗xd4+ ♕xd4 5 ♖xd4 ♗xe6 − draw.

1 ... dxe4+ 2 ♔g2! e3+ 3 ♔g1 ♗f7 And what else?

4 exf7 ♕xc5 5 f8=♕+ ♕xf8 6 f7+ ♕g7+ 7 ♔h2!

But not 7 ♔h1?? ♕xa1+!

and **White wins** 7 ... ♕xa1 8 f8=♕ mate, or 7 ... h5 8 f8=♕+.

In diagram 110, two batteries − one white, the other black, are ready to operate. The difference between them is apparent: the white battery has no real power, because of the white bishop's pin. On the other hand, Black's threat of 1 ... ♔f3+ looks lethal.

From a study by D. Gurgenidze
1st Prize, Polish "40 Years" Tourney, 1985

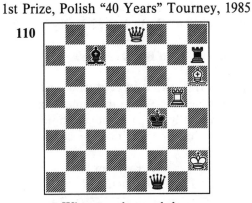

White to play and draw

The rescue lies in the following shocking move: **1 ♕e3+!! ♔xe3+ 2 ♖g3+** Two pieces threaten check, both undefended, both pinned. **2 ... ♔ moves 3 stalemate!**

Benvenutti-Adorni
(Corr), 1910-11

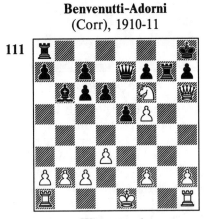

White to play

1 ♖g1! Most probably the simple 1 ♔e2, followed by 2 ♖g1 would be sufficient to win but the actual way that White chose, is undoubtedly more beautiful.
1 ... ♖xg1+

Also hopeless is 1 ... ♕f8 2 ♖g4.

2 ♔e2 ♖g7 3 ♖g1 ♕f8 3 ... ♖ag8? 4 ♕xh7+! mating. 4 ♖g3 e4 5 ♖h3 exd3+ 6 ♔d2 ♕g8

There is no other defence against 7 ♕xh7+.

7 ♘xg8 ♔xg8 8 f6 ♖g6 9 ♖g3 Black resigns.

From a study by L. Silaev
1st Prize, *Shakhmaty v SSSR* 1983

112

White to play and win

A stalemate net has been cast by Black in this study by the Soviet composer: 1 ♖xg1? ♖f8+! 2 ♕xf8+ ♔g6+ 3 ♔g8 ♖h8+! 4 ♔xh8 stalemate!

1 ♖b7! ♖f8+ Forced, apparently leading to the same conclusion as above.

2 ♕xf8+ ♔g6+ 3 ♔g8 ♖h8+ 4 ♔xh8 ♕h1+ 5 ♕h6+!!

A fantastic sacrifice which forces Black to enter an ending of black queen against white rook — which is won for White!

5 ... ♕xh6+ Forced. **6 ♔g8** Strangely, Black is completely without salvation even though he has a 'decisive' material advantage. Against the threat 7 ♖b6 mate there is no remedy, and **White wins**

VI. Dismantling a ready-to-operate battery

In diagram 113, the white battery ♗b3 − ♖d5 is ready to operate but astonishingly the right solution is to dismantle it!

1 ♗d1!!

A 1 ... b4 2 ♗a4, 3 ♗xd7 mate

B 1 ... g3 2 ♗h5, 3 ♗xf7 mate
C 1 ... d6 2 ♗b3, 3 ♖de5 mate
D 1 ... f6 2 ♗xg4, 3 ♖fe5 mate

O. Wurzburg
The Problem, 1914

113

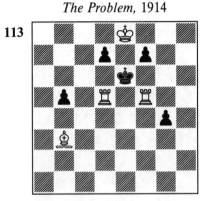

Mate in 3 moves

VII. Intentional entry into a discovered check

From a study by A. Kopnin
2nd Prize, *Shakhmaty v SSSR,* 1964

114

White to play and draw

1 ♔f7!! Just this paradoxical move, which places his majesty exposed to discovered check, brings salvation for White. 1 ♔d7? ♗c4 leaves Black with a decisive advantage.

1 ... ♖e5+

White's last move contained the threats 2 ♘xd5 and 2 ♘g6+ with 3 ♘f8+

2 ♔f6 ♖e6+ 2 ... ♖h5? 3 ♔g6 with the threat 4 ♗c3+.

3 ♔f7 ♖d6+ 4 ♔e8 ♗c6+ 5 ♔f7 ♖d7

What else? 5 ... ♖h6?? 6 ♘g6+ ♔xh7?? even loses: 7 ♘f8+ ♔h8 8 ♗c3+

6 ♔e8!! Repeating the same motif as we saw on the first move.

6 ... ♖d6+ 7 ♔f7 ♗d5+ 8 ♔e8 ♖e6 9 ♔f7 Draw!

12
Creativity — spark of genius, or systematic process of problem solving?

Creativity is surrounded by an aura of mystery and mystical creed. People regard the phenomenon of creativity as resulting from wonderful flashes of inspiration of brilliance, sparks of genius, or acts of magic.

The truth seems, however, to be quite different. As Drucker[16] points out, a successful and innovative trial is usually the product of the careful application of systematic thought rather than any sudden brainwave.

Simon[5] too, opposes the tendency to surround the creativity phenomenon by the nimbus of mystery. According to him, there is no need to assume sparks of genius to account for inventions, discoveries and other such works of humanity. They are all products of the human brain, the very same brain which helps us dress in the morning, get to the office and accomplish our daily tasks, as non-creative as they are.

We have already discussed in Chapter One the concepts of convergent and divergent thinking. In spite of the difference between these two ways of thinking, the act of creation could not be accomplished without them being linked and coordinated.

"Day–dreaming and a profusion of scattered thoughts have no value, even to the thinker himself, unless they can be crystalised into some form of a definite conceptual or practical package ... Spontaneity must dwell together with the logical and the organised."[17] Also on the same subject, Drucker states that, in innovation one invests talent, cleverness and knowledge. But above all innovation requires hard work which is both focused and goal orientated. If consistency, diligence and obligation are missing, cleverness and knowledge will be of no avail.

Back to the stages of creative process, mentioned in Chapter One: it seems that the **preparation** stage should be managed in an orderly fashion and based on logical thought. In the **incubation** and **enlightenment** stages, the thought ramifies into many branches: multidirectional search, trial and error, risk taking, activation of imagination, spirit of adventure, spontaneity, non-conformism. After that, it is important, in the **verification** stage, to return to the system and order which were characteristic of the first stage, since all the ideas which have been conjured up and developed must now be tested, weighed and considered with the utmost care.

I. Chess creativity based on a process of elimination of conventional possibilities

In the following position, which of the two kings is the more vulnerable?

Androvitski-Kosa
Hungary, 1970

115

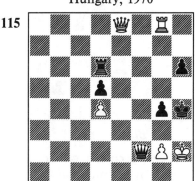

White to play

Black is threatening 1 ... g3+ with an immediate win. White though has no immediate threat. (1 ♕e7+ ♖f6). The reasonable lines of attack are to apply pressure to g4 (which is currently only protected by the black king) or to remove, in some way, the black queen from her position on the second rank, hence releasing the g-pawn from the pin and allowing the advance g2-g3+.

A short analysis proves that these trails are not realisable, but further thought will provide an additional (unpredictable) line of action: **1 ♕e5!** ♖f6 1 ... ♕f6? 2 g3 mate; after 1 ... g3+ 2 ♖xg3 ♖f6 3 ♖h3+ White wins quickly **2 ♕g5+! Black resigns.**

In the position in diagram 116, a move such as 1 ... g1=♗ seems particularly strange, but a systematic analysis of the alternatives reveals that this is the right move:

1 ... g1=♛? 2 ♜d7+ ♚g6 3 ♜g7+! with stalemate.

1 ... g1=♜? 2 ♜xe3, and the ending is drawn.

1 ... g1=♞+? 2 ♚h2 ♞f3+ 3 ♚g3 and Black is lucky to have 3 ...♞d2, holding the draw.

1 ... ♚ moves? 2 ♚h2 and White wins.

Chan-Depasquale
Laoag (z), 1985

116

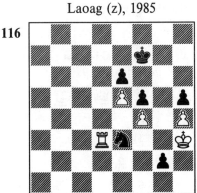

Black to play

The move **1 ... g1=♝!** only occurred to Black after he ruled out the conventional possibilities by elimination. The continuation was **2 ♜d7+ ♚e8 3 ♜h7 ♞d5** and **Black won** after a few more moves.

The following study is an example demonstrating how a systematic and logical analysis is an essential part of the creative process.

Before we examine the possibilities open to White we will note that, among the black camp, only his king is able to move.

Other moves lose immediately: 1 ... bxc6? 2 bxa6, or 1 ... ♝xb5? 2 cxb7.

It's worthwhile to try to 'race' the white king to capture the c7-pawn. A check on the variations shows that this is problematic: 1 ♚f6 ♚f4 2 ♚e7 ♚e5 and here 3 ♚d8 ♚d6 4 ♚c8 ♝xb5! 5 cxb7 ♝a6 and Black wins, or 3 ♚d7? ♝xb5! and again, White doesn't achieve his aim.

A different plan, such as 1 bxa6? bxa6 2 ♚f6 a5 clearly fails as Black is ahead in the pawn race.

The solution comes to light when we try to combine the two plans, the journey to c7 and the capture on a6. Each one on its own is not enough but the application of the combined plan is crowned with success.

From a study by V. Evreinov
1962

117

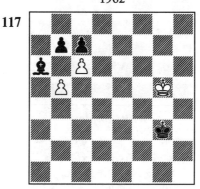

White to play and win

1 ♔f6 ♔f4 2 ♔e7 ♔e5 3 bxa6! bxa6 4 ♔d7 a5 5 ♔xc7 a4 6 ♔d7 a3 7 c7 a2 8 c8=♕ a1=♕ 9 ♕h8+! and wins.

This is another proof that the creative process does not involve, necessarily, the finding of revolutionary moves that were not previously known. There are many instances where the **enlightenment** can be expressed as a fresh organisation of known elements.

In the position shown in diagram 118 White played the obvious move 1 ♘b8 and waited patiently for his opponent's resignation — 1 ... ♘xb8 2 ♕xb8+ costs a whole rook, and 1 ... ♘f8 2 ♘c6 is worse still. The Spanish grandmaster pulled from his sleeve the reply 1 ... ♗e3!, with the main threat 2 ... ♕xf3+ 3 ♖xf3 ♖g1 mate.

Lost in the complexity of the situation, White searched for a path to victory, but in vain. In the end, after long thought, he played 2 ♕xd7+ ♔f8 3 ♕d8+ (3 ♕d6+ ♔g7 4 ♖g2+ ♔h6! and Black wins!) 3 ... ♔g7 4 ♕f6+ (4 ♖g2+?? ♕xg2+) 4 ... ♔f8 5 ♕d8+, settling for a draw.

It was only half a year later that a reader of the British journal, *Chess,* found the correct follow-up[18] 2 ♕c6!! The non-capture is a move which isn't likely to be taken into account. Black is helpless against the

Hutchings-Del Corral
Barcelona, 1975

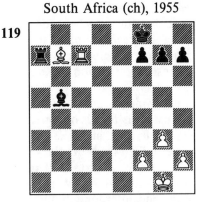

White to play

threat 3 ♕c8+ ♔e7 4 ♘c6 mate, as shown in the following variations: 2 ... f6? 3 ♕xe6+; 2 ... ♔e7 3 ♘xd7 ♗xf2 4 ♕d6+ ♔d8 5 ♘f6+ ♔c8 6 ♕c6+ ♔b8 7 ♘d7+; 2 ... ♔f8 3 ♘xd7+ ♔g7 4 ♖g2+ ♔h8 5 ♖xg8+ ♔xg8 6 ♕c8+ ♔g7 7 ♕f8+ ♔g6 8 ♕g8+ and 9 ♕g2.

Louis-Peenes
South Africa (ch), 1955

119

Black to play

In this position the material equality and the small number of pieces hint at a draw. Even though the white bishop is temporarily pinned, an attempt to take advantage of this by 1 ... ♗a6? will be answered by 2 ♖c8+ releasing the pin and leading to a draw.

1 ... ♗e8!! By means of this move Black prevents a check on the back rank and puts White in a *zugzwang*. The bishop and the rook can't move without loss of material. **2 ♔f1?** This loses. It is unclear whether 2 h4 g6 3 ♔h2 h5 would have changed the outcome. **2 ... g6 3 ♔e1 3 ♔g2?? ♖xb7! 3 ... ♔g7 4 ♖c8**

Black threatened ... ♗b5-a6, with a win of material. By means of the text move White slips out of the pin on the seventh *rank*, only to find himself in a pin on the b-*file*[19]. **4 ... ♗d7 5 ♖b8 ♗a1+ 6 ♔d2 ♖b1!** With the unstoppable threat 7 ... ♗c6. White jumped from the frying pan into the fire ...

7 ♔e3 ♗c6 8 ♗xc6 ♖xb8 White resigns.

II. A creative discovery through despair

Averbakh-Spassky
USSR, 1956

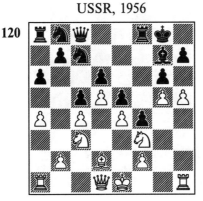

120

Black to play

In the game between the two Soviets, Black handled the opening of the game poorly and found himself in a very difficult position. White has a clear plan — to concentrate all his heavy pieces on the h-file for a crushing attack. Against this, counterplay by Black on the queenside or in the centre is ruled out. Black's next move can be regarded at best as a brilliant burst of inspiration and trickery, or, in more realistic terms, as a desperate attempt to salvage something in the full knowledge that any other continuation will result in certain defeat.

1 ... ♘c6! 2 dxc6 bxc6

In return for the knight Black has a potentially mobile pawn centre, a jumping off point for the knight on e6, and the open b-file for his rook. This certainly isn't sufficient compensation, but as said above, he did not have any other choice.

3 ♘h4 Preferable is 3 a5 followed by 4 ♘a4. **3 ... ♕e8 4 hxg6 hxg6 5 ♕g4 ♖ab8 6 ♘d1 ♘e6 7 ♖a3 ♘d4 8 ♖ah3 ♕f7 9 ♗c3 ♖fe8 10 ♖1h2 ♕xc4 11 ♘xg6 ♖e6 12 ♗xd4?** **♖xg6 13 ♕f5 ♕e6 14 ♕xe6+ ♖xe6 15 ♗c3 d5** Black has considerably improved his chances, and after other adventures, the game ended in a **draw.**

Dr. O. Bernstein-Amateur
Stockholm, 1906

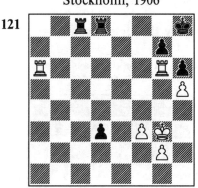

121

White to play

White's position here appears to be resignable. The further advance of the d-pawn (which can't be stopped) will cost him a whole rook. The only chance for counterplay is 1 ♖a7 d2 2 ♖gxg7, which fails due to 2 ... ♖g8!

Despite all this, White is saved from defeat by wondrous means: **1 ♖gd6! d2 2 ♖ac6!!**

What can Black do? White is threatening 3 ♖xd2! **2 ... ♖b8 3 ♖b6! ♖a8 4 ♖a6!** He renews the threat, without let up, at every move. White saved a position that was already beyond despair! **Draw.**

III. Creative chess based on psychological elements

The next three diagrams illustrate a form of creative chess that does not rest so much on an analysis of the chess position as on a deep understanding of human nature.

A falling off in alertness after long periods, a non-objective evaluation of a position, an incorrect distribution of allotted time, loss of patience and so on — none of these are 'pure' chess factors but they do have direct implications upon the outcome of a chess battle.

Peresipkin-Chekhov
Minsk, 1976

122

White to play

Black is in a passive position, and, taking advantage of his opponent's natural desire to demonstrate any kind of activity, White sets a sly trap: **1 a3! ♗b2?**

A seemingly active move, but abandoning the h2-b8 diagonal was exactly what White hoped for. **2 ♘d6!! Black resigns.**

2 ... exd6 3 cxd6 wins a rook, while any other move would allow 3 ♘e8, with or without a check, winning.

In the game shown in diagram 123 the Argentinian grandmaster played very provocatively, tempting his opponent to initiate an attack. **1 ... ♔h8!? 2 a3 ♘g8** The beginning of a general retreat. **3 ♘f1 f6 4 ♘g3 ♗h6 5 ♘f1** White does not commit himself and, as yet, refuses to be coaxed into the attack.

5 ... ♕g7 6 ♗c2 ♖ae8 7 ♕d2 ♘d8!? 8 ♖ad1 ♗c8!? Further provocation. "I'm not doing anything", he proclaims. "Do you want to attack me? Then please, go ahead!"

9 ♘g3 ♘e6 10 b4 ♗xe3 11 ♖xe3 ♘h6 12 ♘e2 ♘f7 13 ♘h2 ♘h6 New heights of provocation — Black proceeds to shift his knight back and forth.

14 ♖e1 f5! 15 exf5 ♘xf5 16 ♗xf5 gxf5 17 f4?! Finally White's patience

Cabrilo-Barbero
Yugoslavia, 1987

123

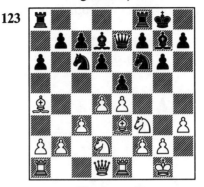

Black to play

breaks **17 ... ♖g8 18 g3?**

Having seduced White into weakening his position, Black wakes up from his trance and initiates a very strong attack. **18 ... exf4! 19 ♘xf4 ♘xf4! 20 ♖xe8 ♕xg3+! 21 ♔h1 ♗e6!! 22 ♖8xe6** Otherwise 22 ... ♗d5+ will be decisive. **22 ... ♘xh3! 23 ♘g4**

Black threatened, *inter alia*, 23 ... ♕g1+.

23 ... ♕xg4 24 ♖f1 ♘f2+!! White resigns. He soaks up a mate after 25 ♕xf2 ♕h3+ 26 ♕h2 ♕xf1.

Zuckerman-Mengarini
Philadelphia, 1971

124

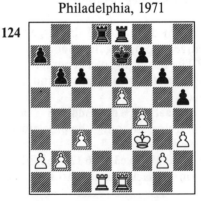

Black to play

And finally — something which testifies on the cruelty of the *Game of Kings*.

From the first moves of the Zuckerman-Mengarini game, Black systematically exchanged off piece after piece with the aim of forcing a draw. From the diagrammed position he continued with this policy.

1 ... ♖xd1 2 ♖xd1 ♖d8 3 ♖xd8 ♔xd8 4 ♔e4 ♔e7 5 g4 hxg4 6 hxg4 ♔d7 This position is, of course, a 'dead draw', but White tries to make something out of nothing.

7 b3 ♔e7 8 ♔f3 ♔f8 9 f5 g5 10 ♔e4 ♔e7 11 b4 ♔d7 12 a4 ♔c7 13 ♔d4 ♔b7 14 c4 a5

A critical moment. White lost his alertness to danger during the game and only thought in terms of a draw or a win. Black takes advantage of this by setting a devilish trap. **15 bxa5 c5+ 16 ♔e4??** Which White falls right into! 16 ♔c3 or ♔d3 were enough to draw. **16 ... ♔a6!! 17 axb6 ♔xb6** and Black wins!

The continuation was **18 ♔d3 ♔a5 19 ♔c2 ♔xa4 20 ♔c3 ♔a3 21 ♔c2 ♔b4** and **White resigns.**

13
Chess Creativity in Action

So far we have examined creative episodes — original ideas at the beginning of the game, exceptional tricks in the middlegame and new discoveries in the ending. In this chapter we move on to consider examples of a genuinely creative approach to the game as a whole.

The following contests are quite dissimilar to other chess battles (and not one of them is like the other ...) and an impression is created that none of the players involved has read a chess book or is familiar with the modern principles of the game ...

Game 1: **Kuzmin-Dorfman**, *USSR (zonal) 1978*

A game which does not feature any development of pieces, strategical thinking or long-term planning. Right from the beginning a crazy race develops as each side captures material and desperately attacks the other's king (over half of the moves in the game, 23 in number, are check!)

In an analysis of the game, the late IM Moshe Czerniak[20] wrote, "a game full of sacrifices, in which all the chess records of boldness were broken; after each sacrifice the reader would ask himself: Which side wants to win?"

1 e4 c5 2 ♘f3 d6 3 ♗b5+ ♘c6 4 0-0 ♗d7 5 ♕e2 g6 6 e5 dxe5 7 ♘xe5 ♘xe5 8 ♕xe5 ♗xb5 9 ♕xh8 ♗xf1 10 ♕xg8 (diagram 125)

10 ... ♗xg2 11 ♔xg2 ♕d5+ 12 ♔g1 ♕g5+ 13 ♔f1 ♕h5 14 ♘c3 ♕xh2 15 ♘d1 ♖c8 16 d3 c4 17 d4 ♕h1+ 18 ♔e2 ♕h5+ 19 f3 ♖c6 20 ♘f2 ♖e6+ 21 ♗e3 ♕h6 22 ♘g4 ♖xe3+! 23 ♔f2! ♖xf3+ 24 ♔xf3 ♕h3+ 25 ♔f4 f5?

25 ... ♕h4! is correct (with the threat of h5) which forces 26 ♔f3 ♕h3+ with a draw. Now White has the opportunity for a counter-attack.

26 ♘f6+! exf6 27 ♖e1+ ♔d7 28 ♕f7+ ♔c6 29 ♕xc4+ ♔d6 30 ♕e6+ ♔c7 31 ♕f7+ ♔c6 32 d5+ ♔b6 33 ♖e6+ ♔a5 34 ♕c7+ ♔a4 35 ♕c4+ ♔a5 36 ♕c7+ ♔a4 37 ♕c4+ ♔a5 38 ♕c3+ ♕xc3 39 bxc3 ♔b5 40 ♖xf6 ♗h6+ 41 ♔f3 ♔c5 42 c4 ♗g7 43 ♖e6 ♗f8 44 ♖e8 Black resigns.

Kuzmin-Dorfman
USSR (zonal), 1978

125

Black to play

Game 2: **Hodgson-Speelman**, *British Championship 1980*

Black sacrifices a pawn in the opening, seeking compensation in the enhanced activity of his pieces, particularly the unopposed light square bishop. Later, having allowed the white f-pawn to march on to the sixth rank, he is obliged to retreat his dark-square bishop, rather embarrassingly, to h8.

On his 22nd move, Black succeeded in regaining both material equality and the freedom of his dark-square bishop. However, he immediately sacrifices another pawn, exchanges one strong bishop for a knight, sacrifices the other bishop, makes a quiet move ... and wins.

1 e4 c5 2 f4 ♘c6 3 ♘f3 g6 4 ♗b5 ♗g7 5 0-0 d6 6 ♗xc6+ bxc6 7 ♘c3 ♘f6 8 d3 0-0 9 ♕e1 c4! 10 d4 c5! 11 dxc5 ♗b7 12 f5 ♕c7 13 cxd6 exd6 14 ♕h4 ♖ae8 15 ♗g5 ♘xe4 16 f6 ♗h8 17 ♖ae1 ♘xg5 18 ♘xg5 h5 19 ♕d4 ♕c6 20 ♘f3 ♖xe1 21 ♖xe1 d5! 22 ♘e5 ♕xf6 23 ♕xa7 ♗a8 24 ♘b5 d4! 25 ♘xd4 ♕f4 26 ♘ef3 ♖d8 27 c3 (diagram 126)

27 ... ♗xd4+! 28 ♘xd4 ♕g4 29 ♖e2 ♗xg2! 30 ♖xg2 ♕d1+ 31 ♔f2 ♖e8! 32 ♖g1

There is no defence against 32 ... ♕e1+. For example, 32 ♘f3 ♖e2+ 33 ♔g3 ♕d6+ 34 ♔h3 ♕e6+ 35 ♔g3 ♕g4 mate.

32 ... ♕d2+ 33 ♔g3 h4+ 34 ♔g4 ♕xh2 35 ♘e6 ♖xe6 36 ♕a8+ ♔g7 37 ♖g2 ♕h1 38 ♔f4 ♕f1+ 39 ♔g4 ♖e4+! 40 ♔h3 ♕h1+ 41 ♖h2 ♕f3 **mate.**

Hodgson-Speelman
Great Britain (ch), 1980

126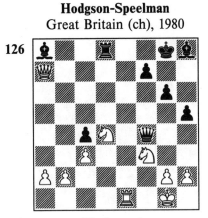

Black to play

Game 3: **Barash-Solan,** *League game, Israel 1984*

Barash-Solan
Israel, 1984

127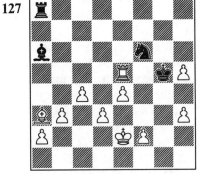

(Variation)

White's first move already hints at an irregular approach to chess, and the continuation only reinforces this impression. White's whole army remains undeveloped, while his queen is rampant in the black camp. So successful is the queen in annihilating the black pawns that in one of the variations (see diagram 127) Black is left completely naked, without a *single* pawn — in sharp contrast to the eight remaining white pawns. As far as we know, this fact in itself has no precedent.

1 g4 e5 2 ♗g2 ♗c5 3 e3 ♘c6 4 ♘c3 d6 5 h3 h5 6 gxh5 ♕g5 7 ♗xc6+ bxc6 8 ♕f3 d5 9 ♘xd5! cxd5 10 ♕xd5 ♖b8? 10 ... ♘e7 is preferable, with an unclear position after 11 ♕xa8 c6.

11 ♕xc5 ♗b7 11 ... ♕g2 12 ♕xe5+! and 13 ♕h2. **12 ♕xc7 ♕g2 13 ♕xb8+ ♔d7 14 ♕xa7 ♕xh1 15 ♔e2!** ♘f6 16 b3 ♖a8 17 ♕b6 ♗a6+ **18 c4 ♕xg1 19 ♗a3! ♕g2 20 ♕d6+ ♔c8 21 ♖g1!** ♕e4 Or 21 ... ♕xg1 22 ♕c6+ etc. **22 d3 ♕b7 23 ♖xg7 ♕d7 24 ♕xd7+ ♘xd7** After 24 ... ♔xd7 **25 ♖xf7+ ♔e6 26 ♖e7+ ♔f5 27 e4+ ♔g5 28 ♖xe5+** a rare position would have been created (diagram 127).

25 ♖g8+ ♔b7 26 ♖xa8 ♔xa8 27 ♗e7 Black resigns.

Game 4: **Petrosian-Schmidt**, *Skopje Olympiad, 1972*

The former world champion, Tigran Petrosian, was renowned for his unorthodox approach to chess. The following game well illustrates his independent and unconventional thinking. Petrosian breaks the whole repertoire of 'sacred' chess principles: exchanging a bishop for a knight (move 8), giving up castling rights (move 11), straightening his opponent's wrecked pawn structure (move 13) capturing flank pawns with his queen and removing her from the centre of action (move 21), disrupting the pawn formation protecting his own king (move 28).

T. Petrosian-Schmidt
Skopje (ol), 1972

128
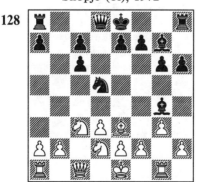

White to play

Petrosian wasn't bothered that the game left a strange impression on his colleagues. The one principle that drove him was to play the *strongest* moves.

1 c4 ♘f6 2 ♘c3 d5 3 cxd5 ♘xd5 4 g3 g6 5 ♗g2 ♘b6 6 d3 ♗g7 7 ♗e3 ♘c6 8 ♗xc6+ bxc6 9 ♕c1 h6 10 ♘f3 ♗h3 11 ♖g1 ♗g4 12 ♘d2 ♘d5 (diagram 128)

13 ♘xd5! cxd5 14 ♘b3 ♕d6 15 f3 ♗d7 16 d4 ♖b8 17 ♔f2 h5 18 ♗f4 e5 19 dxe5 ♗xe5 20 ♕e3 f6 21 ♕xa7 0-0 22 ♖ac1 ♖fe8 23 ♗xe5 ♕xe5 24 ♖ge1 ♖a8 25 ♕xc7 ♕e3+ 26 ♔g2 ♖a7 27 ♕d6 h4 28 gxh4 ♗e6 29 ♖c3 ♕h6 30 a3 ♖d7 31 ♕g3 d4 32 ♖d3 ♗xb3 33 ♖xb3 ♕d2 34 ♔f1 ♔h7 35 ♖b8 ♖e5 36 ♕g4 f5 37 ♕g5 ♖e3 38 ♕f6 **Black resigns.**

Game 5: **Mnatsakanian-Veresov,** *USSR 1968*

The game develops along well known theoretical paths and reaches a position that has been extensively researched and encountered by many thousands of players.

In the position shown in the diagram, Black has a plan involving the continuation 13 ... ♘c4 14 ♗xc4 ♖xc4, followed by ... ♖ac8 and the exchange sacrifice on c3. Meanwhile, White will continue with h5 and ♗h6. A race will develop between the opposing attacks, the winner being the one who gets to the enemy's king first.

That is the 'normal' way to play. However, Veresov finds a totally different plan, which put his pieces in positions that are quite different from those in the acknowledged theory of the Sicilian. He successfully creates something new, using routine and well-chewed materials.

1 e4 c5 2 ♘f3 ♘c6 3 d4 cxd4 4 ♘xd4 g6 5 ♘c3 ♗g7 6 ♗e3 ♘f6 7 ♗c4 d6 8 f3 0-0 9 ♕d2 ♗d7 10 ♗b3 ♕a5 11 0-0-0 ♖fc8 12 g4 ♘e5 13 h4

Mnatsakanian-Veresov
USSR, 1968

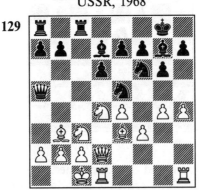

Black to play

13 ... ♖c4!? 14 ♗xc4 Black threatened 14 ... ♖xd4! and 15 ... ♘xf3.
14 ... ♘xc4 15 ♕d3 b5 16 ♘b3 ♕a6 17 ♗d4? e5 18 ♗f2 b4 19 ♘d5 ♘xd5
20 ♕xd5 ♗c6 21 ♕d3 ♗b5! 22 ♘d2 22 ♕d5 ♕xa2! 23 ♕xa8+ ♗f8. 22 ...
♘xb2! 23 ♕d5 ♘d3+! 24 ♔b1 ♕a3! White resigns.

Game 6: **Dobkin-Czerniak**, *Israel (ch) 1955*
Black handles the opening in dubious fashion and is quickly
subjected to a very strong attack. On move 13, White plays a
combination which tears apart the defences of the black king.

In the diagram position a white victory seems to be only a matter of
time, e.g. 15 ... ♖xg6? 16 h4 h5 17 g4 winning.

Black's reaction is based on an amazing concept: he leaves his king
open to discovered check, and initiates a massive attack on the
opposite wing during which his c-pawn develops a brilliant career,
charging forward to promotion in double-quick time.

When White fails to find a convincing culmination of his own
attack, he falls victim to a barrage of tactics.

1 e4 d6 2 d4 ♘f6 3 ♘c3 g6 4 ♘f3 ♗g7 5 ♗g5 h6 6 ♗e3 0-0 7 h3 ♘bd7?!
8 ♕d2 ♔h7 9 0-0-0 a6 10 ♗d3 b5 11 e5 b4 12 ♘e2 ♘d5 13 e6! fxe6 14
♘h4 ♖f6 15 ♘xg6

Dobkin-Czerniak
Israel (ch), 1955

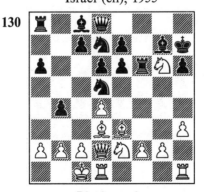

130

Black to play

15 ... c5! 16 ♘f4+
Or 16 ♘xe7+ ♔h8 17 ♘xd5 (after 17 ♘g6+ ♖xg6 18 ♗xg6 ♕a5
19 ♗xh6 ♗f6 20 ♔b1 c4 and Black's threats are the more dangerous)

17 ... exd5 18 c3 c4 19 ♗c2 a5 with a double-edged game. Maybe 16 ♘e5+ ♔h8 17 ♘g4 was best, preventing Black's 19th move.

16 ... ♔h8 17 ♘h5 ♕a5! 18 ♔b1 18 ♘xf6? ♕xa2 19 ♕e1 ♗xf6. **18 ... ♖b8! 19 ♔a1** 19 ... ♘c3+ was threatened.

19 ... c4! 20 ♘xf6 20 ♗xc4? ♘5b6 **20 ... cxd3 21 ♘xd7 dxe2 22 ♘xb8 exd1=♕+ 23 ♖xd1 ♘xe3 24 ♕xe3 ♕c7 25 d5! exd5**

25 ... ♕xc2? 26 ♕c1 saves the knight as 26 ... ♗xb2+?? fails to 27 ♕xb2+!

26 ♕e2 e5 27 ♘xa6 ♕b6 28 ♘xb4 ♕xb4 29 ♖d3 ♗a6 30 ♕d2 ♕xd2 31 ♖xd2 d4

The *mêlée* is over. As the dust settles it becomes clear that Black's advantage is decisive.

32 f3 d5 33 ♔b1 e4 34 ♔c1 ♗e5 35 ♔d1 e3 36 f4 ♗xf4 37 ♖d3 ♗xd3 38 cxd3 ♗d6 39 ♔e2 ♔g7 40 a4 ♗b4 White resigns.

14
How to Develop Chess Creativity?

Nowadays, many chess players display a pragmatic approach to life in general and to chess in particular. They will not hear of any new idea or accept any suggestion, unless there's something in it for them. It seems to be a sign of the times. Vision and ideals are in retreat, materialism and pragmatism in the ascent.

This being so, this work would be incomplete were it not to deal with the question of how the previously mentioned ideas can be applied to the reader's own style of play.

We have already claimed in the Preface that chess creativity can be developed. We shall now attempt to furnish the reader with some practical advice:

I. Awareness of psychological blocks deterring creativity

A. L. Simberg[21] classified the psychological factors which deter and hinder a creative approach.

Some of the blocks are on the **perceptual** level. For example, the difficulty of isolating the problem facing us; or the inability to perceive the relationship(s) between the different elements of the position.

Other blocks to creativity are to be found on the **cultural** level: blind faith in the authorities, particularly their printed works; the treatment of imagination and fantasy as childish play of no importance.

Blocks of the third kind are those on the **emotional** level. Lack of confidence, fear of failure and the quest for belonging – all these things predispose people to rely on their customary habits in familiar surroundings.

Perceptual blocks tend to dull the subtance of the problem facing us. Cultural blocks limit our imagination, inquisitiveness and courage, while emotional blocks are irrational fears and phobias which hinder us from taking an independent and original course of action.

As Simberg has pointed out – **awareness of the existence of these blocks is conditio-sine-qua-non to overcoming them.**

119

II. Correct definition of the problem

Modern researchers[22, 23] claim that even more important than *problem-solving*, is the skill of *problem-finding*, that is the *ability to pose the right questions.*

Thus, creative thinking may be defined as the ability to discover new problems, never before formulated.

Frequently, people are unable to correctly define their problems, be it because they lack the schemes or methods for arriving at correct definition, or because they rush into planning and concrete calculation and do not allot time enough to define the problem.

Inaccurate definition or identification of the task facing us may cause distortions in planning and in the search for alternative actions.

If the task is defined as the destabilisation of the opponent's pawn formation, it should be tackled differently from the task of capturing one of the opponent's pawns. In the first case, all the immediate resources would be used to weaken the opponent's pawns, and only in the long-term, ways and means will be examined to exploit this weakness. On the other hand – in the second case – the player will concentrate his attention on the variants promising short-term material gains; this may cause him to forgo the initiative or even to weaken his position in order to achieve that task.

For example, diagram 30 tempts us to translate the requirement, White to win, to the alternate wish, to retain the a-pawn. This task is unachievable. We have therefore to redefine the task.

One of the ways to win is by mating attack and this is attainable without the a-pawn.

It follows:

A   Various definitions of the problem lead to different decisions during play.

B   **If a problem is not solved, it is recommended that it be redefined from a different angle; thus the prospects of spotting new and promising ideas are improved.**

III. Tolerance to unorthodox ideas

Anybody who has tried to propose offbeat and seemingly eccentric ideas to an alien public, probably remembers well the cool reception of the audience. This disparaging and deprecative response to any unusual thought is so deeply ingrained in us, that we quickly condemn any contradictory ideas even within ourselves without anybody watching us.

This dismissal of ideas — without even examining them — is detrimental to any chance of creative development. Contained within the previous chapters are numerous positions where many strange and even absurd stratagems were performed — all this originality stems from players who, having once conceived of these ideas did not rush to discard them before checking.

Even if the device formed in our brain is unsuitable in its raw form, after processing and rearrangment it might be of better use to us (see for example diagrams 73 and 76).

We must never harm the preparation stage of the creative process by exposing it too soon to judgement and evaluation. We must hoard ideas, not kill them!

IV. Integration of known elements

Some researchers of the creative phenomenon claim that any new development or beginning of creative thought rests on already existing knowledge.

Mednick[24] considers creative thinking to be a reprocessing of elements and connections into new compounds. The basic concept of this theory regards all creative thinking as composed of new combinations of existing ideas. These ideas are being regrouped in a manner helpful to the recognition of previously unnoticed connections and consistencies. W. J. Gordon has built a whole theory based on this conception, naming it 'Cynectics.'

Diagram 117 gives a good example of creative solution composed of linking conventional ideas. In order to produce creative ideas, **the player must exhaust thoroughly his acquired knowledge and review it in various combinations — until successful.**

V. Widening of horizons, avoiding specialization

Some players specialize in a very narrow area of the *Game of Kings* and neglect its other aspects. Becoming an expert in, say, the MacCutcheon variation of the French defence, while disregarding other openings, or mastering technical endgames while neglecting their artistic counterparts — all this leads the player to know all about nothing, and, in fact, he knows nothing.

There is, of course, some advantage in the monotonous repetition of the same openings and schemes, in as much as they make the player an expert in certain positions. This system, however, might drain the creative source of a chess player – his games become alike and the potential range of new ideas shrinks.

Another trap for the specialised player has been described by the Soviet trainer Vladimir Zak[25]. He observed how many players who have a prodigious knowledge of the openings – often based on rote learning – would display a drastic deterioration in their play once that stage was over.

The chess player who wishes to avoid such pitfalls has to become familiar with a wide range of ideas and schemes, and to make himself adroit with all aspects of the game.

This is the true meaning of what the literature of the game terms, the universal chess-player: He has no grey areas whose paths he has not yet trodden and whose mysteries remain unknown to him.

Acquaintance with a rich repertoire of plans, formations and ideas enhanaces the chance of the right thought striking the chess-player at the right moment.

It is recommended to the player who wishes to acquire a wide repertoire of experiences, **to diversify the range of openings he adopts in his games and to enter intentionally into uncomfortable situations in order to gain the relevant knowledge and self assurance.**

The Soviet Grandmaster Arthur Yusupov said recently in a press interview:

(I wanted to) "try other kinds of chess. I did so in a few tournaments in my career. I may not have been too successful but afterwards ... you feel better, and you have broadened your possibilities"[26].

VI. Use of Imagination

As children we are brought up to distinguish between the imaginary and the real.

Mixing up fantasy and facts is frowned upon in the world of grown-ups, and the child learns quickly to restrain his imagination.

We meet the results of this restraint in various areas of everyday life. Inventors, discoverers and pioneers are rebuffed by resentment and contempt, alleging, "These are impractical ideas". Stressing the practical side causes players to construct their plans according to the perceived constraints of the position and thus to forgo their full creative potential.

The correct course is – first to define the desirable goals, even if their practicality is faint and the possiblility of their execution remote.

The direction of thinking should be from the whole to the parts and from vision to constraints.

These considerations make it worthwhile to contemplate once again the game Bastrikov-Ragozin (diagram 47).

VII. Criticism and Doubting

Curiosity is considered as a trait to be encouraged in children. Unfortunately, however, there is a big gap between attitudes and behaviour.

In real life teachers tend to make children know their place if they ask too many questions — thus teaching them (indirectly) to obey the agreed rules and conform.

One of the outstanding characteristics of good chess players, is distrust and suspicion[27]. This finding is compatible with the fact that experts in the development of creativity recommend the adoption of a manner of thinking which puts to the test any assumption or statement.

"Who asserted this statement?" "How did he arrive at it?" "Is it valid?"

These are the questions asked by the creative player.

He does not accept prescribed recipes and will not blindly follow the luminaries.

He checks, investigates and gets to the root of the problem on his own.

(In the Grandmaster tournament, London 1980, GM John Nunn adopted the same opening system against Miles as the then world champion, Anatoly Karpov, had used a short time before. Nunn lost and commented, "It's pretty bad when you can't even trust the world champion"[28]. That's right).

VIII. Self disciplined training

It is a well-known fact that one cannot develop one's own skills without a lot of hard work in training.

As the swimmer does not learn to swim by correspondence, but needs to actually practice swimming, so **it is impossible for the chess player to develop his creative-thinking skills without working on proper chess stimulants,** which will enable him to use his imagination.

Self-disciplined training in producing unusual and peculiar ideas must be based on analysis of complex positions that contain a variety of possibilities.

For this task, some study material needs to be compiled. Notice that such could be taken from sources other than games. For instance, some samples from the problem-world can be quite useful.

A form of chess in which one side plays several moves in succession can contribute to the development of a schematic way of thinking. As examples we should mention the field of 'serial problems' (see diagram 131), and a variant 'progressive chess' in which each player makes a series of moves that is numbered one more than the opponent's: White starts with one move, Black answers with two, White makes three successive moves, and so forth[30].

If this is too wild for the reader, he can investigate a more orthodox sub-field, like 'many-movers' (see diagram 132), and discover in it a mine of golden ideas.

J. Retter
3rd Prize, *Feenschach* T. T. 1978

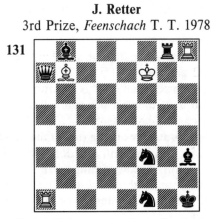

131

Serial Helpmate in three, 3 solutions

Here we face a serial helpmate in three, meaning Black has to make three successive moves in order to enable White, at the end of this series, to deliver mate.

A. 1 ♗h2, 2 ♗g2, 3 ♘d4 — ♖xf1 mate.

B. 1 ♖g1, 2 ♘h2, 3 ♗d7 — ♗xf3 mate.

By now the reader has surely understood the leading principle: Mate becomes possible by getting two black pieces pinned.

C. 1 ♖g2, 2 ♘g1, 3 ♘g3 — ♖xh3 mate.

In diagram 132 the move 1 ♗g6 is the obvious choice, but after 1 ... ♔g8 2 ♕xh7+ ♔f8 it is not clear how White will achieve his aim in the

J. Kriheli
Die Schwalbe, 1981

132

Mate in eleven moves

required number of moves.

Delving into the problem's secrets a little further, we may discover 1 ♗g8?! ♔xg8 2 ♕e8 mate. Black, however, will not be so generous and by 1 ... ♖h2! 2 ♕xh2 ♔xg8 he will parry White's plot.

Let us try to integrate these ideas and execute the mating combination somewhat differently.

1 ♗g6! ♔g8 2 ♕d5+! ♔h8 3 ♕d8+ ♗g8 4 ♗f7 ♔h7 5 ♕d3+!
Repetition of the non-capture motive which occurred on the second move.

5 ... ♔h8 6 ♕h3+ ♗h7 7 ♗g6 ♔g8 8 ♕e6+!
And again.

8 ... ♔h8 9 ♕e8+ ♗g8 10 ♗h7! and mate next move.

IX. The motivational aspect of creativity

It is possible to play creatively only if one wants to. This rather trivial statement must be made in view of the fact that many chess players show no real interest in becoming creative. It appears that even at the higher levels some people do not care about the contents of their games, as long as the bottom line (meaning tournament points) is positive.

Happily, most players do possess that strong human need which reveals itself as a sense of uneasiness about what exists, a feeling of tension and an urge to find solutions (one's own solutions) to the problems.

This is **the will to shape the environment and not to be shaped by it**[31].

A motivated person is willing to make a considerable effort to attain his goals; He shows persistence, perseverence.

When Isaac Newton was asked how he had discovered the law of universal gravitation, he answered simply "By thinking on it continually."[32]

15
Test Your Creativity

The following positions are designed to train the creative thinking of the reader. To reach the solution he must apply the thinking tools that are covered in the previous chapters. Grasping the solution holistically, casting doubt on established principles, searching for a variety of ideas from different sources, placing pieces in unusual positions, being alert to subtle details, etc.

Ivanov-Grigorov
USSR, 1987

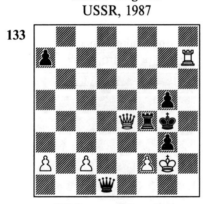

White to play and win

Picture a mating position ...

S. Kozlowski
Ksiega Jubilee Ty, 1938

134

White to play and draw

A paradoxical idea ...

Bogolyubov-Amateur
Stockholm, 1919

135

White to play and win

Taking advantage of weak dark squares ...

From a study by
Kuznetsov & Sakharov, 1976

136

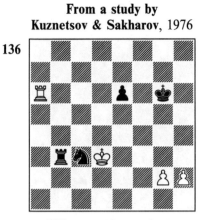

White to play and win

The one who laughs last wins ...

Christiansen-Seirawan
USA, 1978

137

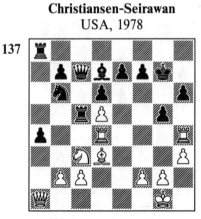

White to play and win

A quick transfer from one wing to the other ...

G. Slepian
1st Honourable Mention *Chess and Draughts,* 1981

138

White to play and win

Queens are designed to be sacrificed ...

Behting-Romashkevich

139

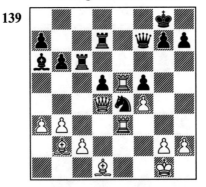

White to play and win

If only it were possible to reconnect the white rooks ...

Gufeld-Tarve
Tallinn, 1969

140

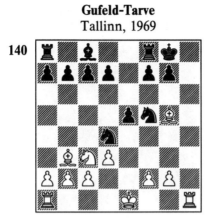

White to play and win

A mating attack in slow motion ...

A. Lewandowski
Commended, *Szachy* 1976

141

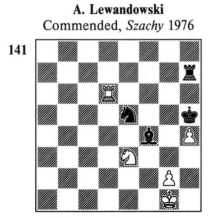

White to play and draw

Chess martyrdom ...

From a study by J. H. Marwitz
3rd Prize, KNSB 1976

142
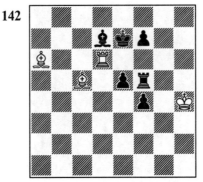

White to play and win

A kamikaze attack ...

Solutions to exercise positions

133. A calculation of single steps is no good. You have to envisage different mating patterns and only then try to fathom out how to achieve them.

1 ♖h4+! ♚xh4 1 ... gxh4 2 ♕g6 mate 2 ♕h7+ ♕h5 2 ...♚g4 3 ♕h3 mate 3 fxg3+ ♚g4 4 ♕d7+ ♖f5 5 ♕d1+ and **mates**.

134. 1 ♖a1 ♚g2 Intending 2 ... ♗f1 and 3 ... h1=♕. White cannot prevent this, but he can still save the battle. The source of his salvation lies in the next move which seems so silly that it is easily overlooked without examining it carefully.

2 ♚h8!! Enabling Black to promote with check!

2 ... ♗f1 3 ♖a7! h1=♕+ 4 ♖h7 wins the queen, and a **draw**! If the white king had still been on g8, then 4 ... ♗c4+ and the black queen is freed.

135. The squares d6 and f6 are particularly weak since there is no black bishop to control them. A white knight on e4 could easily finish Black off very quickly, except that this square is under the control of the black d-pawn. Look again and you will find enlightenment.

1 ♗e4!! dxe4 It makes no difference if the offer is declined, e.g. 1 ... ♘c6 2 ♗xd5!

2 ♘xe4 ♘8d7 3 ♕c3 ♕e7 4 ♘f6+ ♘xf6 5 exf6 ♕f8 6 ♕c7 ♘d7 7 ♘d5! exd5 8 ♖he1+ ♘e5 9 ♖xe5+ ♗e6 10 ♚b1!

An essential preparatory move. If 10 ♖1xd5? immediately, 10 ... ♕h6+ and 11 ... 0-0 and Black is safe.

10 ... ♖d8 11 ♖1xd5! ♖xd5 12 ♖xd5 ♗xd5 13 ♕c8 mate

136. 1 ♚c2 ♘e4! 2 ♖xe6+ ♚xb3? ♘c5+ 2 ... ♚f5 3 ♖xe4!

So White is two pawns up and victory seems assured.

3 ... ♖h3!! Threatens 4 ... ♖xh2, and if 4 gxh3 ♚xe4, White cannot win even with two extra pawns.

4 ♖e2!! ♖xh2 5 g4+ and **White wins**.

137. 1 ♖xh6!! ♚xh6 2 ♖h4+!! The rook is taboo. If 2 ...gxh4 3 ♕c1+ ♚h5 4 ♕d1+ ♚h6 5 ♕d2+ ♚h5 6 ♕e2+ ♚h6 7 ♕e3+ ♚h5 8 ♕f3+ ♚h6 9 ♕f4+ ♚g7 (9 ... ♚h5 10 ♕xf7+, mating) 10 ♕g5+ ♚f8 11 ♕h6+, mating.

2 ... ♔g7 3 ♖h7+ ♔f6 Or 2 ... ♔f8 3 ♕d1 and ♕h5. 4 ♖h6+ ♔g7 5 ♖h7+ ♔f6 White repeats moves to gain time. 6 ♘e4+ ♔g6 6 ... ♔e5 7 b4+! ♔xd5 8 bxc5 with a decisive advantage.

7 ♕d1! g4 Capturing the rook results in mate after 8 ♕h5+

8 ♕d2 ♖xd5 9 ♕h6+ ♔f5 10 ♖xf7+ ♔e5 11 ♕g7+ ♔e6 12 ♖f6+ ♔e5 13 ♖xd6+ ♔f4 14 g3+ **Black resigns.**

138. 1 ♕f1+!! ♔xf1 2 ♗b5+ ♕c4!! After 2 ... ♔xe1 3 ♘c2+ White wins in prosaic fashion.

3 ♘xc4!! Not 3 ♗xc4+ ♔xe1 4 ♘c2+ ♔d2 5 ♘d4 ♔c3 and Black draws.

3 ... fxe1=♕ 3 ... ♔xe1? 4 ♘e3 and wins. 4 ♘e3++ ♔f2 5 ♘g4 **mate!**

139. 1 ♗h5! ♕xh5 Forced. 1 ... g6?? 2 ♖5xe4 or 1 ... ♕f8?? 2 ♖e8 2 ♖3xe4! Taking advantage of the double pin, on the d-file and on the fifth rank. White's combination resulted "only" in exchanging bishop for a knight, but now the threat 3 ♖e8+ is decisive. 2 ... ♕g6 3 ♖e8+ ♔f7 4 ♕xd5+! and **Black resigns.**

140. 1 ♘d5 ♘xb3 Not 1 ... f6?? 2 ♘xf6 (or ♘e7) mate! Now Black expects to be able to organise his defence after 2 axb3 f6.

2 ♘f6+!! gxf6 3 ♗xf6 ♘g7 4 axb3

Black, with material advantage and the right to move, is helpless against White's plan of doubling rooks on the h-file.

4 ... ♖e8 5 g4 ♖e6 6 g5 b6 6 ... ♖xf6! 7 gxf6 ♘e6 would offer stronger resistance. 7 ♔e2 e4 8 d4 e3 9 f3 d5 10 ♖h4 ♗a6+ 11 c4 dxc4 12 ♖ah1 and **Black resigns.**

141. 1 ♘d5! ♘f3+ 2 gxf3 ♖g7+ Not 2 ... ♗xd6 3 ♘f6+ but now White looks dead-lost ...

3 ♖g6!! Unbelievable.

3 ... ♖xg6+ 3 ... ♔xg6 4 ♘xf4+ ♔f5+ 5 ♘g2 draws.
4 ♔h1 ♗ moves 5 ♘f4+ ♗xf4 **stalemate!**

142. 1 ♔g4! ♖f6+ White really asked for it ... in fact the move was forced in view of the threat 2 ♖xd7+. 1 ... ♗e6 loses nicely to 2 ♖xe6++ ♔xe6 3 ♗c8+ ♔d5 4 ♗e7! 2 ♖e6++! And after one blinks several times, the truth dawns upon us: it is mate next move.

More Creative Chess

Various Themes

16
Fresh possibilities in old settings

Creative ideas often manifest themselves in common-place positions. In diagram 143, the combination of White's rook on d1 and bishop on a5 suggest the move ♖d8 mate. Should a black piece hinder this mate (say a bishop on f6), we are likely to think in terms of removing that piece.

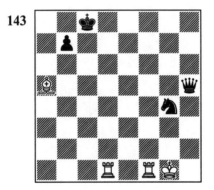

143

Likewise, Black's queen on h5 and knight on g4 on the right side of the diagram are geared towards ♕h2 mate.

In the following positions, the players tackled such routine settings in an original manner:

From diagram 144, **1 ♖xe5+! fxe5**

1 ... ♕xe5 2 ♗f4 ♕d5 3 ♕e1+ ♔d8 4 ♖xd5+ cxd5 5 ♕a5+; or 2 ... ♕e7 3 ♗d6 ♕f7 4 ♖e1+ leads to defeat.

2 ♗d8!! A star move.

2 ... ♕f7 3 ♕d6 Intending, inter alia, 4 ♗e6. If 3 ... ♗f8 4 ♕xe5+.

3 ... b6 4 ♗g5 Finally returning to the well-known idea of mate with the *queen* on d8. **Black resigned.**

Fanenschmidt-Stohl
Germany, 1993

144

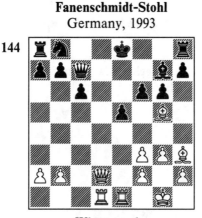

White to play

Tesla-Maryasin
USSR, 1985

145

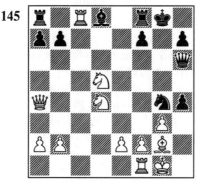

Black to play

On his last move, White captured a black bishop on c8, expecting swift victory, e.g. 1 ... ♖xc8 2 ♘f5 ♕g5 3 ♕xg4!

1 ... hxg3 2 ♘f3

Another line is 2 ♖fc1 gxf2+ 3 ♔f1 ♕h4!! 4 e3 (4 ♘f3 ♘h2+ wins the queen) 4 ... ♘h2+ 5 ♔e2 ♖xc8 6 ♖xc8 ♕g4+ and Black wins.

2 ... ♘h2!! Surprisingly, the h2 square is occupied by the *knight*.

3 ♖fc1 ♖xc8 4 ♖xc8 ♘xf3+ 5 exf3 gxf2+ 6 ♔f1

If 6 ♔xf2, then ♕h4+! wins a whole rook. In the game Black

implemented this idea in a different way:

6 ... ♕d2 7 ♕g4+ ♔h8 8 ♕b4 ♕e1+! 9 ♕xe1 fxe1=♕+ 10 ♔xe1 ♗h4+ and **Black won.**

Pecker-Maryasin
Israel (open ch) 1995

146

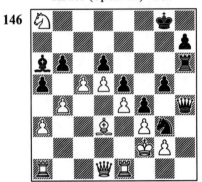

White to play

Black has sacrificed a great deal to achieve this threatening position. White should play 1 ♗xa6!, vacating d3 for his king after 1 ... ♘xe4++ 2 ♔e2. Instead he played **1 ♔g1?** apparently willing to split the point after 1 ... ♕h1+ 2 ♔f2 ♕h4 with a repetition.

But Black used the idea shown in the previous diagram (not surprising, since it was conceived by the same player!) to great effect: **1 ... ♘h1!!** with the double threat of 2 ... ♕f2 mate and 2 ... ♘f2.

2 ♖e2 ♘f2! 3 ♕d2 (3 ♕e1 is more stubborn) **3 ... ♘xd3 White resigned.**

17
Versatile Pieces

The scope of each chess officer is vast: we usually exploit but a fraction of its potential.

Realising the full spectrum of an officer's power is a source of constant satisfaction for composers and players alike.

M. Hlinka
1st Prize, Pravda (Bratislava) Ty. 1990-91

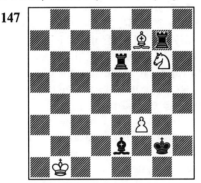

147

White to play and draw

To accomplish his task, White must win a whole rook.

1 ♘f4+ ♔g3

1 ... ♔xf3? (1 ... ♔h2? 2 ♗xe6 =) 2 ♘xe6 ♖xf7 3 ♘g5+ =.

2 ♘h5+! ♔h4

Black must chase the knight, otherwise White will play 3 ♗xe6 =.

3 ♘xg7 ♗d3+, preparing for ... ♖e7, which would fail if played immediately, on account of 4 ♘f5+. This is already the third fork, and there are more to come!

4 ♔b2 ♖e7 5 ♗c4! ♖b7+ Naturally, 5 ... ♗xc4? allows 6 ♘f5+.

6 ♔c3 ♗xc4 7 ♘f5+ with **8 ♘d6** the final fork, drawing.

An impressive knight-tour-de-force: ♘g6-f4-h5-g7-f5-d6.

139

Yuchtman-Palatnik
Odessa, 1964

148

White to play

1 ♘xa7! ♘xa7 2 ♖e5 ♕g6

The alternate defence 2 ... f5!? 3 ♕xd5+ ♔h8 4 ♕xa5 ♘c6 5 ♕b5 ♘xe5 6 ♗xe5 is hardly cheerless from Black's point of view.

3 ♖g5! ♕e6 4 ♖e1 ♕d7 5 ♖xd5 ♕a4 All forced. Watch White's rook dance along the fifth rank. Now the same rook strikes a deadly blow:

6 ♖g5! ♖cd8 6 ... ♗e6 is countered similarly, while 6 ... ♕d7 is no longer available, because of 7 ♖xa5.

7 ♖xg7+! ♔h8 Or 7 ... ♔xg7 8 ♗h6+ ♔h8 9 ♕g5, mating.

8 ♗e5! Prepares a mortal "mill" after 8 ... ♖xd2 9 ♖xf7+ ♔g8 10 ♖g7+ ♔h8 11 ♖g5+.

8 ... f6 9 ♕h6 Black resigned.

On 9 ... ♗f5, simplest is 10 ♖e7, mates. The rook has performed miracles along the fifth rank, the seventh rank and the g-file.

From diagram 149, **1 ♕g6!**

1 ♕xg7? fails to 0-0-0!. After the text move, 1 ... fxg6 invites the humorous 2 0-0 0-0-0 3 ♖c1 mate!

However, it is the other variations which illustrate our theme:

The threat: **2 ♕h7! 0-0-0 3 ♕c2 mate** demonstrates the zig-zag manoeuvre along the b1-h7 diagonal.

1 ... b3 2 ♕xg7 0-0-0 3 ♕c3 mate is an "echo" of the previous line; **1 ... ♖c8 2 ♕e4+ ♔d8 3 ♕e7 mate** integrates diagonal and vertical movements; Finally, **1 ... b5 2 ♕e4+ ♔d8 3 ♕xa8 mate** combines motion on two crossing diagonals: b1-h7, and h1-a8.

A. Selivanov
64, 1990

149

White to play and mate in three

18
The return of the phoenix

Like the legendary bird which surfaces from the dead, moribund pieces (long buried in our minds) have been known to rise from the ashes — only to live and battle again.

A notable example of this race is the bishop:

Csom-Flesch
Hungary, 1966

150

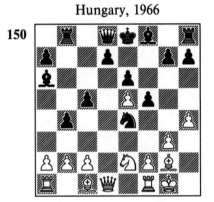

White to play

White ignored the pin on the a6-f1 diagonal and played **1 ♘f4?! ♗xf1 2 ♕h5+ g6! 3 ♘xg6** to be astounded by **3 ... ♗e2!!** which forced immediate resignation (4 ♕xe2 hxg6; or 4 f3 ♘xg3).

The apparently doomed ♗f1 proved a decisive factor in warding off the attack.

From diagram 151 White launched a flawed combination with **1 ♖xd4**, intending to meet 1 ... ♖xd4 with 2 ♘e8, winning the queen, on account of the mate threat.

Black defended coolly with **1 ... ♗xg2!**. Now 2 ♔xg2 ♖xd4 3 ♘e8 is refuted by 3 ... ♕b7+!; So White interpolated **2 ♖d7!** but after the

Gashibaizov–V. Zhuravlev
USSR, 1971

151

White to play

shrewd **2 ... ♗f3!!** was forced to capitulate. **3 ♖xc7?** allows mate; Otherwise he is left with decisive material disadvantage.

The following position was reached after the moves **1 e4 d5 2 exd5 ♘f6 3 ♘c3 ♘xd5 4 ♘f3 ♘c6 5 d4 ♘xc3 6 bxc3 ♗g4 7 d5!? ♘e5 8 ♘xe5!? ♗xd1 9 ♗b5+ c6 10 dxc6**

Goldenberg–Shevaldonnet
Bordo, 1982

152

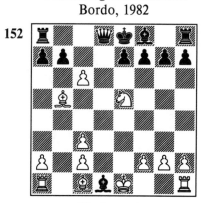

Black to play

The same sequence of moves had already been played in the game Fedorov–Chernin, Minsk 1980, which continued **10 ... ♕d5? 11 cxb7+**

♔d8 12 ♘c6+! and White won.

In the present game, the black player discovered a way to resuscitate his lame bishop:

10 ... ♗e2!!

Threatening the bishop on b5 and intending 11 ... ♕d1 mate. The point is revealed after 11 ♔xe2 ♕d5 12 cxb7+? ♕xb5 with check!; White should have settled for 11 c7+ ♗xb5 12 cxd8=♕+ ♖xd8, with positional advantage for Black. Instead, he faltered with 11 ♔xe2? ♕d5 12 c4 ♕xe5+ 13 ♗e3 and after 13 ... 0-0-0 the game was soon over.

19
Incarceration

T. J. Smith–Morton
(Corr) England, 1954

153

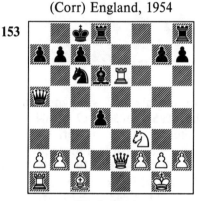

Black to play

1 ... ♕h5 2 ♗d2? Missing Black's threat.

2 ... d3! 3 ♕e3 Not 3 cxd3? ♘d4!, winning. Here 3 ... dxc2 is good enough, but Black is after bigger things.

3 ... ♘d4! 4 ♖xd6 The only move. 4 ♕xd4? ♗xh2+; Or, worse, 4 ♘xd4? ♕xh2+ is losing.

4 ... ♘xf3+!! A long-range winning plan. The obvious 4 ... ♘e2+ 5 ♔f1 ♖xd6 is less effective, on account of 6 ♕xa7! ♖a6 7 ♕e3.

5 ♕xf3 ♕xf3 6 ♖xd8+ An intermediate move, after which White remains a piece ahead. But Black saw farther!

6 ... ♖xd8 7 gxf3 dxc2 8 ♗c1 The ending after 8 ♖c1 ♖xd2 9 ♔g2 g5 or 8 ♔f1 ♖xd2 9 ♔e1 c1=♕+ 10 ♖xc1 ♖xb2 does not leave much hope.

8 ... ♖d1+ 9 ♔g2 b5 White's two officers are imprisoned, and hence, powerless. If he remains passive, Black will win by simply advancing his queen-side pawns, and if necessary, bring his king for help. The game ended: **10 b4 a5 11 a3 c5 12 a4 cxb4 White resigned.**

145

Timman-Adams
Belgrade, 1995

White to play

White won a pawn, but his ♘a7 is caught in his enemy's camp.

1 ♘d5 ♖e8 2 ♘b6! ♗e6 3 ♘c6+ ♔c7 4 ♘d4! ♔xb6 5 ♘xe6 ♖xe6 6 ♖d8 Black is completely tied up, his material advantage does not tell.

6 ... ♖e7 In the game Black lost in a more prosaic manner: 6 ... h5 **7 ♖ad1 f5 8 exf5 ♖eh6 9 ♖b8+ ♔c7 10 ♖dd8 ♖d6 11 ♖bc8+ ♔b7 12 ♖xg8 ♖xg8 13 ♖xg8** and Black resigned.

7 ♖ad1 g5 8 ♖b8+ ♔c7 9 ♖dd8 ♖g7 10 ♔f2 and Black is helpless against the white king's march to the queen-side, sweeping the chain a6-b5-c4.

A. Herbstman & L. Katsnelson
Honourable mention, *Chess in Armenia*, 1975

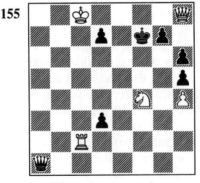

White to play and win

From diagram 155, **1 ♖c5 ♛a8+ 2 ♔xd7 ♛xh8 3 ♖f5+ ♔g8 4 ♘g6** Expecting 4 ... ♛h7 5 ♖f8 mate. Black mobilises his only reserve: **4 ... d2! 5 ♖f1 d1=♛+ 6 ♖xd1 ♛h7 7 ♖g1!**

The queen is kept in exile. The end is tragi-comic: **7 ... ♔f7 8 ♖f1+!** **♔xg6 9 ♖f8! White wins.**

20
Peculiar batteries

The following scheme represents ordinary batteries:

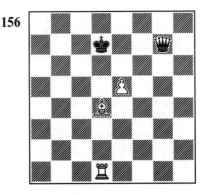

156

1 ♗c5+ activates the battery's base (♖d1) against the black king;
Similarly, 1 e6+ clears the bishop's diagonal, focusing on the enemy's queen.

An ordinary battery comprises two pieces of the same colour. The rear piece has the longer range; its action is temporarily neutralized; when the front piece moves, it unravels the full potential of the rear piece.

The pair of pieces that constitute a battery can be rook and knight, bishop and pawn, queen (directed diagonally towards the target) and rook, etc.

The existence of other, less conventional, batteries was first noted by the prominent study-composer T. B. Gorgiev. He showed that a battery may consist of two pieces with a similar action-range (diagram 157).

1 ♖d4 1 ♖xe5? stalemates.

1 ... ♖e4! 2 ♖d8 The immediate 2 ♖dd7? is answered by 2 ... ♔e1 3 ♖e7 ♖e2+! =.

148

From a study by T. B. Gorgiev
1967

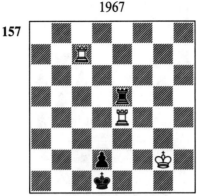

White to play

2 ... ♖e8! 3 ♖dd7! Now 3 ... ♔e1? loses to 4 ♖e7+ ♔d1 6 ♔f2.
3 ... ♖e7! A paradoxical battery of identical pieces is activated:
4 ♖xd2+! ♔xd2 5 ♖xe7 and wins. Insufficient is 4 ♔f2 (4 ♖xe7?
stalemate) 4 ... ♖f7+! 5 ♔e3 ♔e1.

Over the years, I've noticed several uncommon batteries in over-the-board chess. It is not surprising that players tend to overlook them.

Yudasin-Kramnik
Wijk aan Zee (candidates), 1994

White to play

In this position White played 1 ♕xd6? and lost after 1 ... ♘f5 2 ♕c7 e3 3 ♖xe3 ♕xe3! (4 fxe3 ♘g3+ mates).

Both players were under the impression that **1 ♘xd6 ♖h5 2 ♖xe4** is refuted by **2 ... ♘f3**

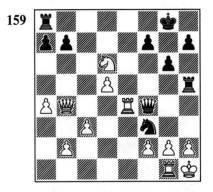

159

However, what is beyond the scope of the front piece in the battery (3 ♖xf4?? ♖xh2 mate), is within the range of the backward piece: **3 ♖e8+!! ♖xe8 4 ♕xf4 wins.**

Surely, an ordinary battery would have easily been spotted by the very strong protagonists.

We have seen "curious" batteries operating on files; they can cross diagonals, too.

Lane-Velikov
Toulouse, 1990

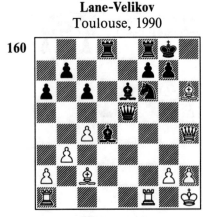

160

White to play

1 ♖xf6? ♗f2!!

1 ... ♗xa1? (or 1 ... ♕xf6? 2 ♗g5) 2 ♗xg7 mates. But having vacated the diagonal for the queen, the stray bishop has created the threat 2 ... ♕a1+. **White resigned.**

Agur-Balshan
Israel (junior ch.), 1965

161

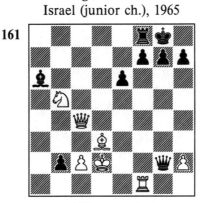

White to play

White resigned in this position, envisaging 1 ♔e3 ♕xf1 2 ♗xf1 b1=♕.

While White's position was far from cheerful, his reasoning was faulty: on **1 ♔e3 ♕xf1??** (better is 1 ... ♕xh2) comes **2 ♗xh7+!! ♔xh7 3 ♕xb1**.

Once again, we see a battery of similar-range pieces. What cannot be accomplished by the bishop is achieved by the queen, although they both operate diagonally.

Bibliography and References

1. CZERNIAK, M. *The History of Chess*
   Mizrachy, 1963. (Hebrew)
2. KOTOV, A. *Train like a Grandmaster*
   Batsford, London, 1981
3. BRONSTEIN, D. & SMOLYAN, G. *Chess in the Eighties*
   Pergamon, Oxford, 1982
4. ANASTASI, A. *Psychological Testing*
   Macmillan, New York, 1976
5. SIMON, H. A. *The Creative Manager*
   Nihool, 1988 (Hebrew translation)
6. LANDAU, E. *Creativity*
   Cherikover, 1973 (Hebrew)
7. KARPOV, A. *Chess at the Top*
   Pergamon, Oxford, 1984
8. KERES, P. & KOTOV, A. *The Art of the Middlegame*
   Penguin, 1964
9. KOTOV, A. *Think like a Grandmaster*
   Batsford, London, 1975
10. DE GROOT, A. *Thought and Choice in Chess*
    Mouton, 1965
11. EVANS, L. & HOCHBERG, H. *How to Open a Chess Game*
    RHM Press, Great Neck, NY, 1974
12. SIMON, H. A. *Rationality as Process and as a Product of Thought*
    American Economical Review, 68, 1978
13. PLESSET, K. *Taking the Plunge*
    Chess Life, 7/1980, p. 43-44.
14. KEENE, R. & LEVY, D. *Chess Olympiad Skopje 1972*
    Batsford, London, 1973
15. GREKOV, N. *Soviet Chess*
    Capricorn Books, New York, 1962

16. DRUCKER, P. *Discipline of Innovation*
Harvard Business Review, 5-6/1985 p. 67-72
17. LAVI, Z. *On the Education to Creativity and on Convergent Thinking*
Hahinooch, 1971 (Hebrew)
18. PIASCIK, S. *Readers' Letters*
Chess, 6/1976, p. 303
19. MILESCU, M. *Practical Game and Composition*
Schachmat, 1975, p. 105 (Hebrew)
20. CZERNIAK, M. *The Pieces are meant to be sacrificed*
Schachmat, 1978, p. 147 (Hebrew)
21. SIMBERG, A. L. *Creativity at Work*
Industrial Education Institute, Boston, 1964
22. CZIKSZENTMIHALYI, M. C. *Motivation and Creativity*
New Ideas in Psychology 6 (2); Pergamon, Oxford, 1988
23. DE BONO, E. *Letters to Thinkers*
Penguin Books, 1988
24. MEDNICK, S. A. *The Associative Basis of the Creative Process*
Psychological Review, 69, 1962, p. 220-232
25. ZAK, V. *Improve Your Chess Results*
Batsford, London, 1985
26. GEUZENDAM, D. T. *Artur Yusupov — Interview*
New in Chess, 1/1988, p. 58-60
27. AVNI, A., KIPPER, D. A. & FOX, S. *Personality and Leisure
Activities: An Illustration with Chess Players*
Journal of Personality & Individual Differences, 1987, p. 715-719
28. HARTSTON, W. R. *The Phillips and Drew Tournament 1980*
British Chess Magazine, 1980, p. 325
29. STEIN, M. I. *Stimulating Creativity (Vol. 2)*
Academic Press, 1975
30. DICKINS, A. *A Guide to Fairy Chess*
Dover, New York, 1971
31. TAYLOR, I. A. *Psychological Sources of Creativity*
Journal of Creative Behaviour, 1976, p. 193-202
32. WESTFALL, R. S. *Newton's marvellous years of discovery and their
aftermath: myth versus manuscript*
Isis, 71, 109-121, 1980

Index of Players and Composers

Numbers refer to diagrams